Welcome to
Indonesian

A beginner's survey of the language

by Stuart Robson

TUTTLE PUBLISHING
Boston • Rutland, Vermont • Tokyo

Published by Tuttle Publishing, an imprint of Periplus Editions (HK) Ltd with editorial offices at 153 Milk Street, Boston, Massachusetts 02109 and 130 Joo Seng Road #06-01/03 Singapore 368357.

Library of Congress Control Number: 2003112845
ISBN 0-8048-3384-2

Printed in Singapore

Distributors

North America, Latin America & Europe
Tuttle Publishing
Airport Business Park
364 Innovation Drive
North Clarendon, VT 05759-9436, USA
Tel: (802) 773 8930
Fax: (802) 7736993
Email: info@tuttlepublishing.com
www.tuttlepublishing.com

Japan
Tuttle Publishing
Yaekari Building, 3F
5-4-12 Osaki, Shinagawa-ku
Tokyo 141 0032, Japan
Tel: (03) 5437 0171
Fax: (03) 5437 0755
Email: tuttle-sales@gol.com

Asia Pacific
Berkeley Books Pte Ltd
130 Joo Seng Road #06-01/03
Singapore 368357
Tel: (65) 6280 1330
Fax: (65) 6280 6290
Email: inquiries@periplus.com.sg

CONTENTS

Introduction

All the languages of this world are interesting and worth studying. But obviously they are all different, and are interesting for different reasons. All of them are a means of communication, be it in an oral or a written form, with our fellow human beings around the globe, and communication, with the mutual understanding this brings, has never been more important.

Anyone who wishes to become acquainted with Indonesia and Indonesians, in whatever capacity, will inevitably need to do this through the Indonesian language. So the study of Indonesian is a worthwhile project, as well as one that brings a high level of satisfaction without too many tears. This is because we do not have to leap the hurdles of a difficult script or a complicated sound-system, such as are found in the case of many other languages. One can go straight to learning vocabulary, thinking about how to compose sentences, and putting such knowledge into practice in the various situations where people meet and talk.

Further, one's use of Indonesian will improve to the extent that one can deepen this knowledge with an understanding of what expressions are appropriate in a given setting, what cultural and social assumptions underlie what we say and how we say it, and how the language fits into its linguistic and historical context.

This little book aims to introduce the reader to the Indonesian language not by creating a course, with grammar and exercises, but by describing it from various points of view, such as telling what it is related to and how it has developed, and on this basis saying where some of its words originate, as a means of familiarization with some common examples. After that the description moves on to talk about the kinds of words one would expect to meet, and how they can be put together as sentences, before providing a few examples of journalistic prose as well as some more literary specimens, in order to give a feeling for the language and whet the appetite for further exploration of this fascinating subject.

And so, *Welcome to Indonesian*!

Acknowledgements

The maps were provided courtesy of Mr Gary Swinton of the School of Geography and Environmental Science, Monash University.

I am also grateful for the assistance of Mr Basoeki Koesasi and Ms Yacinta Kurniasih of the School of Languages, Cultures and Linguistics of Monash University with finding materials and answering questions.

The editors of *Gatra* kindly gave permission to quote examples of Indonesian prose from their journal.

CHAPTER ONE

What is Indonesian?

Indonesian is "the language of Indonesia," or, in Indonesian, **Bahasa Indonesia**. Indonesia is a country of more than 200 million inhabitants, located in Southeast Asia (see Map 1a). Southeast Asia can be divided into mainland and island parts, and thus Indonesia occupies a large portion of island Southeast Asia, together with the Philippines, Malaysia and East Timor. To the east are the nation of Papua New Guinea and the various smaller states of Melanesia and Polynesia.

The land surface of Indonesia is broken up into a large number of islands, some large and many small (see Map 1b). This feature gives it quite a different nature from a continental country such as the United States or Australia. The largest islands of Indonesia are (from west to east) Sumatra, Java, Kalimantan (Borneo), Sulawesi (Celebes) and the western half of New Guinea, now called Papua Barat (formerly Irian Jaya). There are several seas enclosed within the archipelago of Indonesia, for example, the Java Sea, Flores Sea, Banda Sea and Ceram Sea. And to the south there are the Arafura Sea, Timor Sea and the Indian Ocean, while to the north there are the South China Sea and the Pacific Ocean.

So it is no wonder that sometimes Indonesia has been called, somewhat romantically, **Nusantara**, "The Islands." On the one hand, the seas have allowed the development of hundreds of different ethnic groups inhabiting the various islands, with the result that they have their own languages and cultures, but on the other hand the seas have also provided a highway for sailing backwards and forwards, aided by the regularly alternating winds from west and east, called the monsoons.

Politically, Indonesia is a unitary republic, composed of provinces. Independence from the former colonial power, the Netherlands, was declared on August 17, 1945, and sovereignty formally transferred on

December 27, 1949. The national language is Indonesian, as stated in Article 36 of the Constitution of 1945. It is interesting that this should be a matter actually regulated by law. This was necessary in view of the need to replace Dutch (and Japanese, used during the Japanese Occupation), and also to define the relationship with the many other (regional or ethnic) languages of Indonesia. The elucidation on the above article adds, "In the areas possessing languages of their own which are actively used by the people concerned (for instance, Javanese, Sundanese, Madurese and so forth), these languages will be respected and also cared for by the State. These languages are a part of the living culture of Indonesia."

Thus the adoption and use of Indonesian can be seen as a political statement, to the effect that the nation of Indonesia has one language that all the people possess in common. Indonesian is the language of unity (*bahasa persatuan*). Apart from the obvious political aspect, there is also the practical necessity to have a language that everyone can learn and use, one that is not the monopoly of one group, and in this way serves as a means of communication from one end of the country to the other, "from Sabang to Merauke," as Indonesians are fond of saying—these two towns lying at the western and eastern ends of the nation geographically. Indonesian is therefore taught in all schools and is used by all governmental agencies, as well as the national media.

What is Indonesian? We could begin by disposing of some silly misconceptions that are sometimes heard: it is not a pidgin, and it is not an artificial language. It is indeed a modern language, which fulfils all the functions of such, and yet it also has roots deep in the past. As a first step toward explaining this, we can state that Indonesian is a variety of Malay. The term "variety" does not mean "dialect" in this context. It means that Indonesian is Malay, as adopted and adapted for a special purpose, namely to be the national language of the state of Indonesia.

Malay is a language spoken and used in various parts of Southeast Asia in different forms. It is the daily language of the inhabitants of parts of Sumatra and Kalimantan, as well as the Riau Archipelago, for example, as well as of the Malay inhabitants of West Malaysia, and also the sultanate of Brunei and the Malays of Singapore. In this sense it extends across international borders. A knowledge of Indonesian is thus helpful for learning Malaysian Malay (**Bahasa Malaysia** or **Melayu**) and vice versa—but do not be deceived into thinking that they are identical, as there are also many significant differences. Malay, as the national language of Malaysia, and Indonesian are clearly not the same, despite their similarities and a shared spelling system. Speakers or students of one or the other need to be aware of the differences, which in themselves make an interesting study (see Chapter 5).

MAP 1a: Southeast Asia and surrounding countries

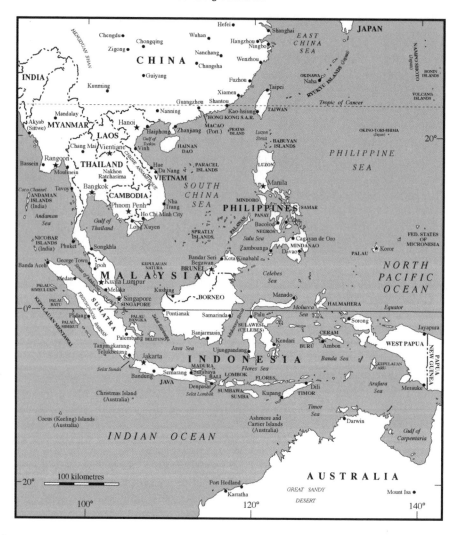

MAP 1b: The islands of Indonesia

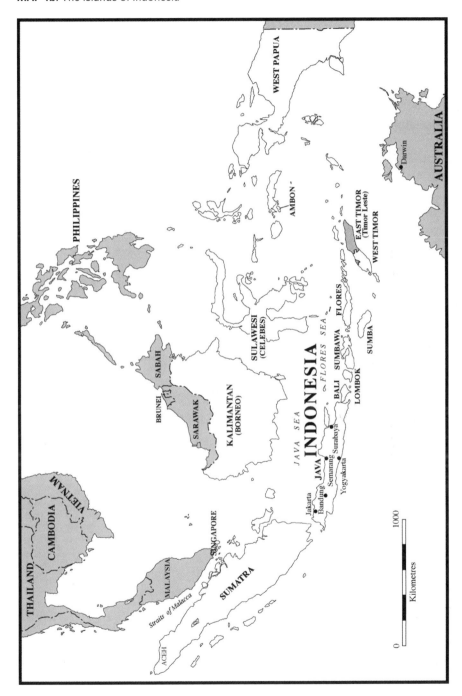

CHAPTER TWO

Bahasa Indonesia as National Language

The very idea of a national language may be unfamiliar to speakers of English in the United States, Britain or Australia, where the wide use and status of English are accepted and unambiguous. There are other countries in the world, though, where the linguistic situation is much more complicated, for example, India, Russia or Indonesia. The concept is closely linked with the idea of the nation state on the one hand, and national and personal identity on the other. The possession of a national language is one of the most important attributes of a state (like a flag or a government), and as well as a practical aspect it also has a symbolic function. In other words, all the citizens of nation X share their national language as a common heritage; it serves to unite them internally, and at the same time to separate them externally from their neighbors, who do not have the same language (or have a different variety of it).

Further, the term "national language" suggests the existence of another language or languages within the nation that are not national. This is certainly the case in Indonesia, and this makes the situation more complex (and interesting!) for the student or visitor.

As mentioned above, Indonesia consists of many islands. These islands have been the home of many distinct ethnic groups for centuries, and these groups possess their own cultures and social traditions, as well as their own languages. These are indeed separate languages (not dialects), and there are about 250 of these in all, the majority belonging to the Austronesian language-family (on this, see Chapter 8). Many, of course, have very small numbers of speakers, but others are quite large. The languages of the various ethnic groups are often called "regional languages" (**bahasa daérah**) because of their association with a particular geographical region, but the terms "ethnic" or "cultural" could also be used.

The main regional (or ethnic) languages being alluded to here are:

- in Sumatra: Acehnese, Batak (in several forms), Minangkabau, and of course Malay
- in Java: Sundanese (in West Java), Javanese (in Central and East Java, as well as many other places due to transmigration), and Madurese (in Madura and parts of East Java)
- in the islands to the east of Java: Balinese (in Bali and West Lombok), Sasak (in Lombok), Sumbawan and Bimanese (in Sumbawa), and so on; and
- in Sulawesi: Buginese, Makassarese and Mandarese in the south, Tontemboan, Bolaang-Mongondo and Gorontalo in the north, and many more.

Given that Indonesia has a national language and that at the same time the nation also consists of groups that have their own language, it should be evident that a person, as member of both the nation and a regional group, is likely to speak two languages. This is an observable fact. But it immediately raises the question of the relationship between the two. Is there a problem? How can the two coexist?

In practice, there is no problem at all, because the national and regional languages have different socio-linguistic functions that normally do not overlap. The contrast lies in both acquisition and use.

A child, born and bred in a particular community, finds him or herself firmly embedded in that social context, and soon imbibes the culture, including language, that exists there and has been passed down through many generations from the ancestors. This language is thus the repository of traditional wisdom in the form of idioms and proverbs, for example, and of culturally significant expressions in the form of performances and rituals, oral history, and literature, in particular oral literature (and in some cases also written).

The regional language is spoken by the whole community, and in fact serves to define the community (and may well have a number of regional varieties—dialects in the proper sense). So it is used in the home, among one's relatives, neighbors and friends. It is intimate—you speak from the heart, as your language has the resources, such as a wealth of terms for local natural phenomena, for the occupations and pastimes that matter to people. It resonates with shared knowledge and experience.

But the child is also a member of another community, the nation. And as such he or she will probably go to school and at least complete primary education. This means that the child will straight away be confronted with a second language, Indonesian, which is the medium for instruction in the classroom. It is then this second language that is generally associated with participation in education, going via secondary right through to tertiary level, and hence with modernization and development in their many forms, such as technology and the media.

At the same time, the national language is also an "arm" of the government, through its essential link with the nation, and this arm reaches into every community through the implementation of official policies, reinforced through the media, in particular television, with its endless reports of ceremonies and the activities of administrators.

While on the topic of education, as a footnote we might add that regional languages, at least a major one such as Javanese, also have a place as a subject in high school, and their importance seems to be growing, perhaps as part of the movement toward increasing regional autonomy, and there also exist publications in regional languages.

Thus an individual who has been to school is going to be bilingual, in the sense of being more or less proficient in two languages. The level of proficiency in Indonesian varies a lot, depending not only on one's schooling but also on whether one lives in town or in the countryside, and what kind of occupation one has. Moreover, there are different varieties of Indonesian, ranging from that taught in schools or used in university lecture rooms to the informal, slangy kind found in the streets. Most people will occasionally watch TV and pick up some Indonesian there too, and on occasions when people of different ethnic origins are likely to be present, Indonesian is always the preferred language, so that nobody is excluded. This is another, very important, function of the national language.

People who move from one region to another, for a job or because of marriage, may well acquire a third language, and those who have secondary education will also have learned some English, while in a religious context Muslims will probably have some familiarity with Arabic. So a person's linguistic repertoire can be quite wide.

When two linguistic codes (methods of communication) are available to a speaker within a community, then that speaker is able to switch from one to the other. Observing when and how a person switches may give us insight into the different functions of the two language codes as means of communication. Studies made so far have focused on the interface between Indonesian and Javanese, perhaps because Javanese is spoken by so many people (around 100 million). This involves taking into account a feature for which Javanese is well known, that is, the existence of formal speech levels—Low (called **Ngoko**) expressing intimacy, and High (called **Krama** or **Basa**) used in situations of formality or social distance (including status difference). There may be situations where a speaker either cannot or does not feel inclined to use honorific forms, and so switches to Indonesian as a neutral speech level. If both speakers are Javanese, however, this way of opting out can create a feeling of distance. Another situation in which a speaker switches to Indonesian is seen to depend not so much on social factors but on the subject matter of the conversation. Indonesian is the natural, normal language for any matters of an official, governmental or technological nature, so if such a topic turns up, then a speaker is likely to move, even in mid-sentence, into Indonesian to explain it.

Predictably, if a speaker is familiar with two languages and thus is able to switch easily, there will be a heavy influence of one language on the other. Such influence can go both ways. Since Independence, many Javanese words have been borrowed by Indonesian, and Javanese sentence structures have had a subtle influence on Indonesian. Some of the words taken from Javanese have been from its literary variant, with the effect of creating new words in Indonesian that are redolent of classical, "high" culture, thereby steering formal Indonesian away from its "democratic," lingua franca roots (on loanwords, see Chapter 9).

Javanese, on the other hand, has been influenced by Indonesian, because all the language development required in the context of modernization has taken place in Indonesian, not Javanese, with the result that the terms for anything relating to modern technology, for instance, are taken from Indonesian, or are the same in Indonesian and Javanese. Thus it might be more accurate to say that such words have *become* Javanese when used in a Javanese context. This is truly an example of "shifting languages."

Indonesian is without doubt the means *par excellence* for interethnic communication in Indonesia. This means that when people from different ethnic backgrounds meet they can communicate immediately in Indonesian. However, a recent study has suggested that when persons have been living in the (Javanese-speaking) community for a long time (as sometimes happens), long enough to be on an intimate footing with their neighbors, they tend to use **Ngoko** with each other to express this relationship, while they have not mastered the **Krama** needed for formal situations, so that Indonesian then shifts into the slot for formal communication, like another level of Javanese.

But there is also evidence of a growing role for a variant of non-formal Indonesian, the Jakarta colloquial, used to express intimacy but without overtones of relative status, in particular among the youth and students, in many locations outside Jakarta (on Jakarta colloquial, see Chapter 6).

The interface between Indonesian and the regional languages is likely to remain an interesting topic for study, as people often move to live in different areas for a time, or may marry a partner from a different area, so that we can observe their linguistic behavior and that of their children. There is a great lack of data on the position outside Java, where regional languages are also being confronted with the growing influence of Indonesian. It has been claimed that the smaller regional languages are being abandoned in favor of Indonesian, presumably so that their speakers can enter the mainstream of modern life. This is clearly quite a different picture from Java, with its overwhelming number of speakers of Javanese and a heavy representation in the echelons of the bureaucracy and elite, especially in Jakarta, the site of much of the linguistic change in Indonesia affecting the Indonesian language.

CHAPTER THREE

A Historical Overview

So Indonesian is a variety of Malay, and is also the national language of a state that only declared its independence in 1945. How can this be explained? To answer the question of how such a thing could have happened, we need to look back into the past. A historical perspective will show how Malay came to assume this important new role as Indonesian.

The earliest written evidence for Malay comes in the form of inscriptions on stone from southern Sumatra. Two of these bear dates, 683 and 684 CE. The inscriptions use a system of writing that originated in South India, but was then used for this early form of Malay, called Old Malay. The texts also contain a number of loanwords from Sanskrit, a scholarly language from ancient India (on loanwords, see Chapter 9). The inscriptions are documents issued by the reigning king of a kingdom centered on southern Sumatra, called Srivijaya. Srivijaya probably controlled a number of Malay-speaking settlements in the region of the Straits of Malacca, as far north as Kedah.

The mention of writing derived from India and of Sanskrit loanwords shows that this kingdom, and others like it in various parts of Southeast Asia, had developed a culture that combined local elements with ones borrowed from Indian civilization. These included the religious system followed at court, namely Buddhism. In fact, Srivijaya was a prominent center of Buddhist scholarship, with the result that Chinese monks visited and stayed there to pursue their studies. Some of these monks took the trouble to learn the local language, which they called *K'un-lun* and which (judging from the inscriptions) must have been a form of Malay.

Srivijaya owed its prominence to the fact that it was located close to busy trade routes linking China and India and passing through Southeast Asia, as well as local trade from the inland. It was probably the Malays themselves who sailed to China, and throughout the region, aboard large ships such as are depicted on the reliefs of the great temple of Borobudur in Central Java. Even at this time, it is possible that Malay was also being used more widely as a trade language. At least it is clear from the presence of inscriptions that Old Malay was known and used in Java, and an inscription in it was found as far away as Manila Bay, in the Philippines.

An Indianized culture continued to exist for some centuries in Sumatra, but the kingdom of Srivijaya was broken up in 1025 by an expedition sent by the Hindu Chola king of South India. Not long after this, Islam gained a foothold in parts of South India, and it was from there that it initially entered the Indonesian area. Again the trade routes were significant, as the people who brought religion had to travel on ships, and these were ships carrying trade goods. The first evidence of the establishment of Islam in Indonesia is found in the extreme west, in northern Sumatra (the present Aceh), when the sultan adopted this new religion. His name is known from a gravestone dated 1297 CE, and the story of the kingdom, Pasai, is told in an early Malay history, the **Hikayat Raja Pasai**.

It is interesting to observe that Islam did not come directly from Arabia (its cradle) or any other part of the Middle East, but from India, in this way repeating the pattern we saw earlier. And again, the new religion did not come by itself, but as part of a whole cultural complex. In the case of Islam, as well as a system of belief and way of life, it meant a quite different method of writing, Arabic script, which was used for the holy book of Islam, the Quran, and all the other works of law and theology. Furthermore, adherence to Islam meant membership of a wide, international "brotherhood," very useful for purposes of trade.

Islam was soon introduced from Sumatra into Malacca, founded about 1400, with the result that this new Malay sultanate (located on the Malay Peninsula on the Straits of Malacca) would dominate the trade passing between China and India, as well as from Java and eastern Indonesia. The trade from eastern Indonesia was particularly valuable, as it consisted of spices (nutmeg and mace) and precious woods such as sandalwood, much in demand as far away as Europe. The many merchants who congregated in this port probably used Malay as a means of communicating (on the evidence of a Chinese-Malay wordlist), and the story of the sultanate was told in another Malay history, the **Sejarah Melayu**. (On classical Malay literature, see Chapter 13.)

Precisely because of these links with eastern Indonesia via trade, Islam was conveyed eastwards from Malacca and became established in the ports there during the 15th century. The spice trade attracted newcomers as well, namely the Portuguese, the first Europeans to enter Southeast Asia. The Portuguese had sailed around Africa and set up bases in India, and from there they decided to capture Malacca as a key point in the trade to the east. Malacca was taken from the Malays in 1511, and from there the Portuguese sailed straight on to the source of the spices in eastern Indonesia. And there they found evidence of the spread of Malay, which is very relevant to our story.

The Jesuit missionary Francis Xavier wrote in a letter from Ambon dated May 10, 1546 that Malay was very common and was written with Arabic letters, which Muslim preachers had taught. Even earlier, in 1521, an Italian named Antonio Pigafetta had visited Tidore in the Moluccas and drawn up a list of words useful for communication there, and these words were Malay. We can conclude that Malay had been brought by Muslims, and followed the trade route.

The Portuguese themselves began to use Malay in their efforts to convert the people to Christianity, as this language was the one understood by local peoples and used between them and outsiders. In this way, Malay had already become a lingua franca in some parts of the archipelago. Thus so far we have distinguished three varieties of Malay: mother tongue Malay, as spoken in several regions of western Indonesia; literary Malay, as used at the courts and for religious purposes; and lingua franca Malay, used over a much wider area, and somewhat simplified through use by different ethnic groups, including foreigners.

A crucial event in our story is the arrival of the Dutch in the Indonesian area. They too were in search of trade, and also were confronted with the Malay language, realizing how important it was for their business. The Dutch established a headquarters at Batavia (the present Jakarta) in 1619. The language used there would not be a local, indigenous one (Sundanese or Javanese), but imported ones, Portuguese and Malay for everyday purposes, and of course Dutch for official records. For diplomatic contacts with Indonesian rulers the Dutch used a form of Malay. Being interested in propagating their form of Christianity, they produced a translation of the Bible—into Malay—in 1731–33 (see Figure 3a and Figure 3b). The Dutch clergyman François Valentijn in 1724 described Malay as "a delightful, excellent, sweetly flowing and rich language," and he distinguished a High Malay (used at court and in matters concerning the Islamic religion), and a Low or Pasar (Market) Malay, used daily and spoken by the masses. It is interesting to note that the Dutch printed the Bible and wrote Malay in roman script (Figure 3c), not Arabic characters, and in this way developed the *third* way of writing Malay (after Indian and Arabic scripts).

When the British encountered Malay in Southeast Asia, they too took an interest in it, and the scholar and administrator Thomas Stamford Raffles collected a large number of Malay manuscripts, some of which are still kept in London.

From the beginning of the 19th century, relations between the Dutch and the Indonesians (beginning in Java, and then extending to the outer islands) intensified, and following the Java War (1825–30) the colonial period can be said to have begun in earnest. Colonial administrators, who were often moved from posting to posting, needed to communicate with local heads, and planters had to deal with traders, and for all these purposes Colloquial Malay was used, as it was simpler to master than the various regional languages (which had in any case scarcely been studied) and was widely understood.

Dutch scholars produced dictionaries and other guides to Malay, and missionaries took its study seriously. In Batavia and such towns where a mixed population lived, Malay was used between the various groups, such as Dutch (including people of mixed descent), Chinese and "natives" of various origins. Curiously, the Dutch officials did not allow themselves to be addressed in Dutch by natives—apparently because that might suggest an equal footing and undermine their prestige. Instead they used Malay, a strange situation in which neither party used their own language. The aristocratic lady, Raden Ajeng Kartini, concluded that Dutch was "too beautiful to be used by a brown mouth."

By the end of the 19th century, Dutch officials had realized the value of Malay as a medium of instruction and also as a means of promoting a feeling of solidarity among the peoples they ruled. The idea of unity through language was already appearing among European administrators, long before it was espoused by the nationalist movement. A definitive grammar of Malay by C.A. van Ophuijsen was published in 1910 (second edition 1915) and this set standards for many decades. Government publications, which had formerly been in Colloquial Malay, were now replaced by ones in an officially sanctioned School Malay that was monitored and considered "good and correct."

During the second half of the 19th century and early 20th century, the Chinese had been very active, writing and publishing in large towns such as Batavia, using the local variant of Colloquial Malay for newspapers, novels and even poetry that were sold cheaply and served to stimulate the practice of reading among the public. Then in the early decades of the 20th century, with the spread of education, ideas of the "uplift of the natives" led to hopes of independence and freedom from colonial rule. Although these were dealt with severely, the leaders of the various organizations managed to spread their ideas among the literate (educated) elite—and for this purpose they chose not Dutch (which they knew very well) but Malay, a language accessible to many. They also did not choose a well-developed language such as Javanese, because its use was limited to one region, in contrast to Malay, which had been carried into every corner of the island world not only by traders but also by colonial administrators. Thus the link between Malay (later Indonesian) and politics was established. Then in 1928 the nationalist movement made the famous declaration of "one country, Indonesia" and "one people, the Indonesian people," who "uphold the language of unity, Indonesian."

Predictions had been made that Malay would come to fulfil this historic function. For example, in 1916 S. Surya Ningrat (Ki Hadjar Dewantara) had foretold that Malay "will in future be the obvious language for all the Indies." This ideal could not be realized for the time being. But in 1942 there came a great shock to the colony: the Japanese Imperial forces invaded and the Dutch either fled or were put into internment camps. The use of Dutch was banned, and the Japanese started teaching their own language, but for the time being use had to be made of another language for communication, namely Malay. In this way, the Japanese Occupation gave Malay (Indonesian) a great start on its new career. The Japanese even allowed a committee to be set up to begin on the task of creating all the new terminology that would be required for the language to function in the modern world, and so they set to work translating Dutch terms into acceptable Malay. (On language development, see Chapter 4.)

The use of Malay by the colonial power itself and its adoption for a political role in the early 20th century provide a clue to the kind of Malay that became Indonesian. This was the Malay that had been used by bureaucrats in government offices for decrees and official letters and by writers in big business houses; here the expressions needed for the various branches of government, the business world and the armed forces had already been molded, often by people who had been educated in Dutch (and perhaps knew better Dutch than Malay), so that we find many examples of words now common in Indonesian that have a Dutch "substratum," in the sense that the Malay/Indonesian term is a hidden translation of a familiar Dutch one (examples will be given later).

Forging the link between political movements and parties and the Malay language was crucial in the emergence of Indonesian, and instrumental in this process were journalists who were politically active and worked on the many Malay-language newspapers that were published in the early 20th century. We observe a process of convergence between the office Malay alluded to above, the lingua franca Malay that had already been used in publishing, and the "good and correct" Malay propagated by Van Ophuijsen's grammar and the government publishing house Balai Pustaka. This process would move in the direction of what is now accepted as standard Indonesian. The print media have continued to play a key role in this, and at the present day should still be regarded as the dynamic cutting edge of the language. (See Chapter 12 for some examples.)

FIGURE 3a: Title page of the Malay Bible translation published in Amsterdam and dated 1731. (From a photocopy kindly provided by Dr Roger Tol, Royal Institute of Linguistics and Anthropology, Leiden, the Netherlands.)

'ELKHAWLU-'LDJADÎD,

'I J A 'i T U,

S E G A L̄ A   S Ǔ R A T

PERDJANDJÎAN BAHÂRUW.

ÂT A S   T Î T A H

S E G A L̄ A   T U W̄ A N   P E M̄ A R E N T A H

K O M P A N I J̄ Â

TERSÂLIN KAPAÐA BAHÂSA MALÂJUW.

Dibendar 'A M̄ I S T E R D A M,

Tertarâ 'awleh R. dàn ÐJ. W E T 'I S T E J N, P E Ñ A R Â ɸ

K O M P A N I J̄ Â.

M D C C X X X I.

FIGURE 3b: Opening page from the Gospel of Matthew, from the Malay Bible translation of 1731–33, showing the spelling system then used for Malay, including the stool-shaped letter devised to represent the Arabic letter *ain*. (Courtesy of Dr Roger Tol.)

'I N DJ Î L U-'L KH U D U S

T E R S Ú R A T 'A W L E H

M   A   T̄   A   J.

FATSAL JANG PERTÂMA.

1 Ûrat 'atſal Ꙅîsàj 'Elmesêth , 'ânakh lâki p Dâ'ûd , 'ânakh lâki p 'Ibrâhîm.

2 'Ibrâhîm per'ânakhlah Jitslhâkh: dàn Jitslhâkh per'ânakhlah Jaꙅkhûb : dàn Jaꙅkhûb per'ânakhlah Jehûdâ, dàn ſegala sûdarânja lâki p.

3 Maka Jehûdâ per'ânakhlah Pérets dàn Zérath deꞩan Támar : dàn Pérets per'ânakhlah HHetſrawn : dàn HHetſrawn per'ânakhlah Râm.

4 Maka Râm per'ânakhlah Ꙅamînadab : dàn Ꙅamînadab per'ânakhlah Nathefjawn : dàn Nathefjawn per'ânakhlah Salmawn.

5 Maka Salmawn per'ânakhlah Bawꙅaz deꞩan Rathâb : dàn Bawꙅaz per'ânakhlah Ꙅawbejd deꞩan Rût : dàn Ꙅawbejd per'ânakhlah Jifjâj.

6 Maka Jifjâj per'ânakhlah Dâ'ûd Sulthân 'îtu : dàn Sulthân Dâ'ûd per'ânakhlah Solejmân deꞩan parampuwan 'îtu , jaꞩ dihûlu deper'isteríkan 'Urijâ.

7 Maka Solejmân per'ânakhlah Rethabꙅam: dàn Rethabꙅam per'ânakhlah 'Abijâ : dàn 'Abijâ per'ânakhlah 'Àsâ.

8 Maka 'Àsâ per'ânakhlah Jehawfjafath : dàn Jehawfjafath per'ânakhlah Jawram : dàn Jawram per'ânakhlah Ꙅazarjâ.

9 Maka Ꙅazarjâ per'ânakhlah Jawtam : dàn Jawtam per'ânakhlah 'Àthaz : dàn 'Àthaz per'ânakhlah HHizkhijâ.

10 Maka HHizkhijâ per'ânakhlah Menafjej : dàn Menafjej per'ânakhlah 'Amawn : dàn 'Amawn per'ânakhlah Jawfjijâ.

11 Maka Jawfjijâ per'ânakhlah Jekonjâ , dàn ſegala sûdarânja lâki p ſakîra p pada wakhtu perpindâhan ka-Bâbel.

12 Maka komedijen deri pada perpindâhan ka-Bâbel Jekonjâ per'ânakhlah SJe'alti'ejl : dàn SJe'alti'ejl per'ânakhlah Zerubâbel.

13 Maka Zerubâbel per'ânakhlah 'Abijûd : dàn 'Abijûd per'ânakhlah 'Eljakhîm : dàn 'Eljakhîm per'ânakhlah Ꙅazawr.

14 Maka Ꙅazawr per'ânakhlah T̄Sadawkh : dàn T̄Sadawkh per'ânakhlah 'Achîn : dàn 'Achîn per'ânakhlah 'Elijûd.

15 Maka 'Elijûd per'ânakhlah 'Elꙅazâr : dàn 'Elꙅazâr per'ânakhlah Matan : dàn Matan per'ânakhlah Jaꙅkhûb.

16 Maka Jaꙅkhûb per'ânakhlah Jûſof mampilej Marjam 'îtu , jaꞩ deri padânja telàh taper'ânakh Ꙅîsàj jaꞩ terſebùt 'Elmesêth.

17 'Adapawn ſakalijen pûpu deri pada 'Ibrâhîm ſampej kapada Dâ'ûd , 'itûlah 'ampat belàs pûpu : dàn deri pada Dâ'ûd ſampej kapada perpindâhan ka-Bâbel , 'ampat belàs pûpu : dàn deri pada perpindâhan ka-Bâbel ſampej kapada 'Elmesêth , 'ampat belàs pûpu.

18 Bermûla mawlid Ꙅîsàj , 'Elmesêth 'adâlah demikijen perînja : kârana tatkâla Marjam 'ibûnja 'itu ſudahlah bertunâꞩan deꞩan Jûſof , maka dihûlu deri pada mâſokh ſatuboh marîka 'îtu

ⱥ

FIGURE 3c: The Foreword to the *Maleische Spraakkunst* (*Malay Grammar*) of G.H. Werndley (1736). He refers to the language as "called Bahasa Jawi by the scholars, and Bahasa Melayu, the Malay Language, in general." (Courtesy of Dr Roger Tol.)

Pag. 1

VOORREDEN,

Behelzende eene Inleiding tot de

MALEISCHE

SPRAAKKUNST.

§ 1. 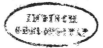E taal, welke wy voor-hebben te verhandelen, wordt onder de geleer-den بهاس جاوي Bahâ-fa Djâwij, *de Djawifche taal*, en in 't gemeen بهـاس ملايو Bahâfa Malâjuw, *de Maleifche taal*, genaamd.

§ 2. Door den eerften naam wordt de Ma-leifche taal van de Arabifche en Perfifche ta-len onderfcheiden, en te gelyk aangewezen, dat deze taal is de gemene en gebruikelyke fpraak, daar de beide andere talen van de geleerden zyn. Dit onderfcheidt wordt ons voorgefteld in het Maleifch boekje, genaamd: مراة المؤمن Mir'âtu-'lmû'min, *de Spiegel van een gelovige*, het welk onder de Muhamme-daanfche Maleiers zeer beroemd is, in wel-kers inleiding de fchryver, na de voorgaan-de loffprekinge aan Godt en den valfchen propheet Muhammed, aldus aanvangt: وبعد

أدڤون كمدين دڠ ابت مكّ ڤدَ هجرة
سريبو سمبيلن تاهن دڠ ڤد هجرة نبي
الله

CHAPTER FOUR

The Development of
Modern Indonesian

From the moment in 1928 when the Indonesian youth movement took its oath to uphold the Indonesian language, the leading figures began thinking about ways in which they could translate this into action. The first Language Congress was held in Solo (Central Java) on June 25–28, 1938, and after hearing a paper given by Amir Sjarifoeddin on "Accommodating foreign words and concepts into the Indonesian language" the congress passed a resolution to adopt foreign words for sciences, and that this work should be done carefully, by submitting it to a body.

Although the formulation is still fairly vague, under this point we can already see what was to become a preoccupation of language planners and practitioners, namely the best way to prepare the Indonesian language for its function as a language capable of being used in all branches of science. Obviously there was an assumption that Malay was not yet developed enough to be able to do this—an idea that may seem odd from the perspective of the 21st century. There was an assumption that foreign words would need to be borrowed in order to create the new terms; it would be Dutch words that the intellectuals turned to, as these were considered appropriate for anything modern or scientific.

Nothing more could be done for the time being, until the period of the Japanese Occupation. At the request of the Indonesians, the Japanese Army's Office of Education set up a Language Committee on October 20, 1942, chaired by Sutan Takdir Alisjahbana. The Committee had three sections: Grammar, Testing new words, and Terms. Takdir and his friends worked away at these projects undisturbed, till they were closed down on April 30, 1945 because of nationalist activities. However, the results of their work were published shortly after the Occupation, in the form of two small volumes. The first appeared in 1945 as the **Kamoes Istilah I Asing-Indonesia** (*Dictionary of Terms I: Foreign-Indonesian*), and the second in 1947 as **Kamoes Istilah II Indonesia-Asing** (*Dictionary of Terms II: Indonesian-Foreign*).

In this context, "foreign" meant Dutch, and the new terms that were discussed and approved by the Committee were sought first in Malay, and after that in other Indonesian languages, and finally in Sanskrit or Arabic. The total number was 7,000, and the terms were very technical.

Following the capitulation of the Japanese and the proclamation of the Republic two days later on August 17, 1945, a period of chaos ensued. The work of the committee was taken up again but it had the opportunity to meet only once, on July 21, 1947, before returning Dutch forces seized its offices, and the Republic moved its capital to Yogyakarta, where it held off the Dutch for some time, during the period known as the Revolution.

As a Dutch scholar, G.W.J. Drewes, remarked in 1948, Malay was teeming with new words that could not be found in the dictionaries, but were to be read in the daily newspapers. They did not come from the **Kamoes Istilah**, but most likely could be found in the Javanese dictionary, as either colloquial or literary terms. If before the war there was a Sumatran period in the development of Malay, then after the war it went through a Javanese period. This was attributed to the removal of the seat of the Republic from Batavia to Yogyakarta and the spread of terms via the press of Central Java.

The system of spelling was the one inherited from the colonial period, but the first Minister of Education, Soewandi, initiated an improvement as early as March 19, 1948, with the replacement of the digraph *oe* with *u*. It was more efficient to use one letter for one sound, and the letter *u* had not been used in the previous system; furthermore, it was a nationalistic step. However, many people still use *oe* instead of *u* in the spelling of their name.

A **Balai Bahasa** (Language Centre) was set up by the Republican administration in Yogyakarta in March 1948, under the Minister of Education and Culture (and the building still exists). This would be the first in a series of several institutions, all with the aim of cultivating and developing language, leading up to the one that exists in Jakarta today. After the Transfer of Sovereignty from the Netherlands to Indonesia at the end of 1949, and the takeover by the Republic in Jakarta, the **Balai Bahasa** now came under a new institute, the **Lembaga Ba-**

hasa dan Budaya (Institute of Language and Culture), which was set up in 1952 as part of the **Fakultas Sastra** (Faculty of Arts) at the University of Indonesia in Jakarta.

In 1959 this was changed to become the **Lembaga Bahasa dan Kesusasteraan** (Institute of Language and Literature), under the Department of Education and Culture. Then on November 3, 1966 it was changed again, to become the **Direktorat Bahasa dan Kesusasteraan** (Directorate of Language and Literature). In 1969 it became the **Lembaga Bahasa Nasional** (National Language Institute), and finally, on April 1, 1975, it became the **Pusat Pembinaan dan Pengembangan Bahasa**, or **Pusat Bahasa** for short, normally translated as "National Language Development Centre," under the Director-General of Culture. This has grown and flourished, and today continues to fulfil an important function in the cultivation and development of language in Indonesia.

Alongside the institutional developments, there were also important publications in the field of language. Again going back to 1948, a monthly magazine appeared, founded and edited by Sutan Takdir Alisjahbana, called ***Pembina Bahasa Indonesia*** (*Cultivator of Indonesian*). This contained articles on questions of language for the information of readers on such matters as grammar, correct usage of words, questions from readers, general articles, and even language exercises. A proportion of the articles seems to have been written by Takdir himself. In September 1950 it had a print run of 15,000 copies, suggesting that it was widely read. It ceased publication around 1957. Takdir had been writing essays on the Indonesian language since the founding of the independent literary journal ***Pujangga Baru*** (*New Poet*) in 1933, as well as fiction, the novel ***Layar Terkembang*** (*With Sails Unfurled*, 1939) being the best known (see Figure 4a). In 1957 Takdir's articles were collected and published as a useful volume under the title ***Dari Perjuangan dan Pertumbuhan Bahasa Indonesia*** (*On the Struggle and Growth of Indonesian*, reprinted in 1988).

Meanwhile, a more substantial journal, ***Bahasa dan Budaya*** (*Language and Culture*), was being published by the **Lembaga Bahasa dan Budaya**, commencing when this was still attached to the **Fakultas Sastra** of the University of Indonesia, beginning in 1952, and continuing up to the present day as a publication of the **Pusat Bahasa**. In the 1950s a **Komisi Istilah** (Terminology Committee) was again set up, probably inspired by the one that existed during the Japanese Occupation. Its results were listed as regular appendices to **Bahasa dan Budaya**. All these lists are from Dutch to Indonesian; the intention was to ensure that there existed Indonesian equivalents for every kind of technical term. The words were divided into sections, for example animal husbandry, military matters, mathematics and physics, education, aviation, agriculture and engineering.Apart from terminology, another matter that continued to occupy the minds of Indonesians during the 1950s was spelling. The Language Congress held in Medan in 1954 urged changes, and ideas began to be exchanged with scholars of Malay in Malaya and Singapore. The Federation of Malaya became independent from the British on August 31, 1957, and in April 1959 a cultural agreement between Indonesia and Malaya was signed, to include matters of language such as spelling. A delegation went to Jakarta and met Sukarno. A joint system of spelling would be created, to be called the **Ejaan Melindo**, but no details were ever announced. Instead, history intervened in the form of Confrontation, when Malaysia became the enemy. Furthermore, politically and economically the early 1960s were extremely difficult years for Indonesia, and people had little time or inclination to think about little things like spelling.

The question only arose again in 1966, after the establishment of the **Orde Baru** (New Order) by Suharto. A spelling commission, chaired by Anton Moeliono then of the **Lembaga Bahasa dan Kesusasteraan**, was set up in May 1966, and a draft proposal was ready by August. This was submitted to the Malaysians, and was agreed and published in 1967. After much debate, it became official on August 17, 1972, and a similar proclamation was made by the Malaysian government, so that both countries would now use the same system of spelling. This new spelling is called the **ejaan yang disempurnakan** ("perfected spelling"), and the details were set out in a little guide called **Ejaan Baru**. The main effect was that in Indonesia the former **dj**, **j** and **tj** became **j**, **y** and **c** respectively, while in Malaysia only the former *ch* became *c*.

At this point, it is interesting to look at Malaysia, as there has been a similar concern with language development there, although this arose at a somewhat later date due to the historical circumstances. An institution called the **Dewan Bahasa dan Pustaka** was established in June 1956 as a small government bureau under the Department of Education in the pre-independence Federation of Malaya. After Independence in August 1957, the new Federal Constitution declared Malay as the National and Official Language, and in 1959 the Dewan Bahasa dan Pustaka Ordinance was enacted, making the **Dewan** an autonomous statutory body under the Ministry of Education. Exactly ten years after independence an Act of Parliament, called the National Language Act 1967, was passed, naming the National Language the sole official language of the country, replacing English. The **Dewan** has had many activities, including an extensive publication program. For example, it published a monthly magazine, called *Dewan Bahasa*. This contains lists of new technical terms, translated from English into Malay. These were formulated by terminology committees in various fields.

The **Pusat Bahasa**, which has its headquarters at Rawamangun in Jakarta, also engages in a wide range of activities. These cover both the Indonesian and regional languages, literature in Indonesian and regional languages, lexicography and terminology. In order to implement this program, it has an extensive program of publications, and provides information to the public on the correct use of Indonesian. An important example of its work in the field of lexicography is the great monolingual Indonesian dictionary, *Kamus Besar Bahasa Indonesia*, a very complete and reliable work produced by a large team and first published by **Balai Pustaka** in 1988.

An example of a publication in the area of terminology is the *Pedoman Pengindonesiaan Nama dan Kata Asing* (*Guide to the Indonesianization of Names and Foreign Words*, 1995), which lists English terms with an Indonesian equivalent, divided into seven sections, for business and finance, industry, sport and art, tourism, communications and telecommunications, personal appurtenances, and property.

It is interesting to make a comparison with other Southeast Asian languages. In the Philippines an Institute of National Language was set up in 1937, when President Quezon declared Tagalog to be the national language. But much has happened since then. In 1971 President Marcos declared that the national language would be known as Pilipino, and in 1986 the new constitution made Filipino the national language, with the intention to create a broader national language in the future, which would include borrowings from other major languages such as Ilocano, Cebuano, Pangasinan and so on. Meanwhile it would still be based on Tagalog, but Tagalog would eventually be just another regional language. I understand that the debate is ongoing.

In Thailand, where there is one main language, Thai, the process of modernization began early with the efforts of HRH Prince Wan Waithayakon Krommun Naradhip Bongspraband, an Oxford graduate and respected diplomat and scholar, who on his return from Europe in 1919 started coining words which were needed for a Thai version of the Civil and Commercial Code, and went on from there. He is said to have created around 300 words, which are now mostly in common use, making use of Pali and Sanskrit. His work in this area has been continued till the present by a Bureau of the Royal Institute, so that Thai has a complete range of terms needed for modern life.

The need for new terms grows by the day, and Indonesian keeps pace with this by either creating a new word or by adopting the English. Some examples from the field of information technology can serve to illustrate this.

ENGLISH	INDONESIAN
information technology	*téknologi informasi*
net(work)	*jaringan*
server	*penyedia jaringan*
operating system	*sistém operasi*
software	*perangkat lunak*
application	*aplikasi*
screen	*layar*
memory	*mémori*
access	*aksés*
patch	*perisai* ("shield")

In other cases, an Indonesian term has been devised, but is followed by the English, apparently "just to make sure," e.g.

intégrasi lintas-platform	cross-platform integration
mesin maya	virtual machine
sistém operasi beragam	multi-operating system

And in various other cases, the English word is inserted, but printed in italics, to show that it is still foreign, e.g. *browser, boot manager, desktop, user name, password, download.*

FIGURE 4a: The cover of the original edition (1936) of Takdir Alisjahbana's novel *Lajar Terkembang*, depicting the "sails unfurled." (Asian Studies Research Library, Monash University)

CHAPTER FIVE

Indonesian and Malaysian

From a historical and structural perspective, both Indonesian and Malaysian (**Bahasa Malaysia**) are closely related variants of the same language, Malay. However, we refer to them as separate languages, and they function as the national languages of two separate states. The spelling reform of 1972 had the effect of making the two look the same, as they use an identical writing and spelling system, but on a lexical level considerable differences remain (see the attached list of examples, based on the *Times Comparative Dictionary of Malay-Indonesian Synonyms* by Leo Suryadinata, 1991).

The differences are of various kinds:

- A mere difference in spelling (e.g. Indonesian **coba**, Malay *cuba*);
- A borrowing from Dutch in Indonesian and from English in Malaysian (e.g. Indonesian **klakson**, Malay *hon*);
- A heavy influence of Javanese in Indonesian and Arabic in Malaysian; and
- An independent process of coining terms.

In some cases the same word has a different meaning in each language, leading to great hilarity in some cases, e.g. Indonesian **butuh** "need," and Malaysian *butuh* "penis."

So in answer to the oft-asked question "Are the two languages the same?" we can give an unequivocal answer "No." Although the two may be mutually intelligible in their educated forms, there is still the risk of misunderstanding, or just plain mystification.

The linguistic situations of Indonesia and Malaysia are, after all, quite different. In Malaysia, the Malays, whose mother tongue is Malay, use either an uneducated (kampong) variety, or have an English education and may not have made a serious study of their Malay, even if it is compulsory, whereas the large Chinese community have no interest in Malay as a language whatever, even if they are forced to learn it at school and use it with officials. Although the expressions of administration, for example official forms, are in Malay, the influence of English is nevertheless strong due to the dominant influence of this world language and the colonial past.

At the same time there is a tendency on the part of the Malaysian media to imitate Indonesian in pronunciation and vocabulary (terms such as **demonstrasi** "demonstration" and **reformasi** "reform" come to mind), although there is no observable influence in the opposite direction, perhaps due to the fact that the population of Indonesia is ten times larger than Malaysia's. But despite this tendency, the evidence suggests that Indonesian and Malaysian are not converging at all, but diverging at a rapid rate.

The contrasting situation of Indonesian and Malaysian is brought about not only by their different historical circumstances, namely the British colonial presence in Malaysia and the Dutch one in Indonesia, but also the fact that Indonesian has a large number of regional languages alongside it, chiefly Javanese, a language with a huge number of speakers which represents of reservoir of borrowings, in both its colloquial and classical forms. Whilst Javanese provides Sanskritic formations, deriving from deep in its Old Javanese past, Malay's heritage is the Arabic of Islam. The deep well of spoken Malaysian Malay is the vernacular of the Malay states, while the speakers of regional Malay within Indonesia are relatively lacking in influence, and the analogous source in Indonesia is to be sought in the colloquial of Jakarta (see the next chapter).

The following list shows some contrasting Indonesian and Malaysian words.

INDONESIAN	MALAYSIAN	ENGLISH
akhir	*hujung*	end
alinéa	*paragraf*	paragraph
asrama	*hostél*	dormitory
ban	*tayar*	tyre
bangun:membangun	*bina:membina*	to build
banyak	*ramai*	many

bestik	*bifstik*	beefsteak
béda	*béza*	different
bicara	*cakap*	talk
bisa	*boléh*	can, to be able
bon	*bil*	bill
butuh:membutuhkan	*perlu:memerlukan*	to need
capai	*penat*	tired
coba	*cuba*	to try
ceroboh	*cuai*	careless
darurat	*kecemasan*	emergency
dokter	*doktor*	doctor
formulir	*borang*	form (to fill in)
guru	*cikgu*	school teacher
handuk	*tuala*	towel
hari ulang tahun	*hari jadi*	birthday
ijazah	*sijil*	certificate
informasi	*maklumat*	information
isi	*kandungan*	contents
izin:mengizinkan	*benar:membenarkan*	to permit
jangan	*usah*	don't
juara	*johan*	champion
judul	*tajuk*	title (of book, article)
kacamata	*cermin mata*	spectacles, glasses
kamar	*bilik*	room
kamar kecil	*bilik belakang*	toilet
kantor	*pejabat*	office
kapan	*bilamana*	when?
karena	*kerana*	because
kejahatan	*jenayah*	crime
keluhan	*aduan*	complaint
keponakan	*kemenakan*	niece/nephew
kemudi:mengemudi	*pandu:memandu*	to drive (a car)
klakson	*hon*	horn
kualitas	*kualiti*	quality
kuliah	*syarah*	(university) lecture
mau	*mahu*	to wish, want
médali	*pingat*	medal
minggu	*pekan*	week

pahlawan	*wira*	hero
pesan	*oder*	order
pelajar	*penuntut*	(school) student
pemerintah	*kerajaan*	government
pertama kali	*julung-julung kali*	first time
pérs	*persuratkhabaran*	the press
pipa	*paip*	pipe
panitia	*jawatankuasa*	committee
polisi	*polis*	police
prapatan	*simpang jalan*	crossroads
rahasia	*sulit*	secret
rapat	*miting*	meeting
rekan	*rakan*	colleague
rusak	*rosak*	out of order, broken
soré	*petang*	afternoon
séhat	*sihat*	healthy
sékrétaris	*setiausaha*	secretary
sisa	*baki*	leftover
stéker	*plag*	(electrical) plug
sumber	*punca*	source
suratkabar	*akhbar*	newspaper
terhormat	*berhormat*	respected
tatabahasa	*nahu*	grammar
terusan	*kanal*	canal
tetangga	*jiran*	neighbor
toko	*kedai*	shop
umum	*am*	common, general
warganegara	*rakyat*	citizen
wawancara	*temuramah*	interview

CHAPTER SIX

The Colloquial Dimension: Influence of *Dialek Jakarta*

Indonesian is of course used for both writing and speaking, and within these modes of expression we find variation, depending on such things as the medium, who is being addressed, and the setting. This variation ranges from formal to informal, and these speaking styles or registers are all part of the language. The style of a TV news bulletin is quite different from a chat with a friend, for instance. In writing a letter in English we may vary the tone too, for example: "I write to inform you that…" in contrast to "I'm just writing to let you know that…"—depending on who you are writing to and what the circumstances are. Both are correct, of course, but it is important to know the right way to say something in order to convey the appropriate feeling in a given situation.

Within the informal register, then, spoken Indonesian can also shift from the "good and correct" ideal in the direction of purely colloquial forms, that is, ones which are rarely seen in print but commonly heard, and are typically highly expressive. And the source of these is the language of Jakarta. Being the capital, with not only a large and mixed population but also much of the wealth, Jakarta is the center of everything trendy and thus has a huge influence on the rest of the country, or at least those open to contacts with outside, depending on the extent to which people travel, have family living there, and so on.

The speech of Jakarta has been heavily influenced by, but is not identical with, what is sometimes called **dialék Jakarta** ("Jakarta dialect"), or **omong Jakarta** ("Jakarta speech"). This was once called **Melayu Betawi** ("Batavian Malay"). The origins of this language are to be sought in the lingua franca Malay that began to be used in Batavia in VOC (East India Company) times. During that time a variety of ethnic groups, such as Balinese slaves, were brought to Batavia. After the abolition of slavery, the indigenous communities gradually stabilized and merged, with the result that Malay became a first language (in contrast to a second language). This process took place mainly in the first half of the 19th century, and the language was only really established in the second half. So it should be stressed that this variety of Malay does not represent the dialect of some "original" group of Malay-speakers, either in Batavia or elsewhere. Apart from Malay, the other influences on it were Javanese, Sundanese, Balinese, Dutch and also of course Chinese, via those Chinese who were converted to Islam and absorbed into the indigenous community. This group is still called the **anak Betawi**. As a social group in Jakarta they are today a tiny minority, confined to a few kampongs.

In the post-independence period Indonesians have moved to the capital from all corners of the Archipelago. But by far the greatest influx has been from Central Java. Far from being only out-of-work farmers, such migrants represent the whole social scale, from domestic helpers and laborers at the bottom, right up to bureaucrats, generals and even feudal aristocrats at the top. The language-use of these people is an interesting point for the development of Indonesian. Observations have shown that while the first generation may still use Javanese at home, their children speak the language of the local community with their friends. And this language is not pure school Indonesian, but the natural colloquial language of the region. It is in fact a mix, ranging from Jakarta colloquial on the one hand to standard Indonesian on the other, this mix being constantly varied according to the situation in which they meet and talk.

The Jakarta colloquial is recognizable because of its particular characteristics, which can be summarized under three areas:

1. Word-forms

The system of affixation differs from standard Indonesian (on these affixes, see Chapter 10) in the following ways:
• The prefix **me-** is absent, and different rules of nasalization apply.
• The suffixes **-kan** and **-i** are replaced by **-in**.
• The prefix **ber-** is generally absent.
• The prefix **ter-** is replaced by **ke-**.

Some examples:
nemenin	"to keep someone company," cf. standard **menemani**
nemuin	"to find, meet," cf. standard **menemukan**

2. Sounds

- The vowel *a* is replaced by *e* in a final syllable, e.g. instead of **dapat** ("get") we find **dapet**; instead of **senang** ("happy") we find **seneng**.
- A glottal stop is frequent in final position, e.g. *juga'* ("also").

3. Words

There are also typical, frequent words, such as:

nggak	"no; not" (instead of ***tidak***)
pada	(marking a plural, placed in front of the verb)
sama	"with" (instead of ***dengan***)
kayak	"like" (instead of ***seperti***)
banget	"very" (instead of ***sekali***)
entar, or ***ntar***	"later, soon" (shortened from ***sebentar***, used instead of ***nanti***)
bikin	"make" (instead of ***buat***); and importantly,
gua or ***gué***	"I" (informal), a borrowing from Hokkien Chinese
lu	"you," a borrowing from Hokkien Chinese;

and in particular the emphatic particles, placed after another word:

déh	(from ***sudah***) used with the sense of urging; e.g. ***Begini aja déh, aku bayar 50%, kamu bayar 50%***, "Come on, let's do it this way: I pay 50% and you pay 50%";
sih	with the sense of softening a question or statement; e.g. ***Aku sih tak peduli dia kaya atau nggak***, "In my case, I don't care if he's rich or not"
dong	asserting that "you should know or do what I say," and used almost as an exclamation mark; e.g. ***Kamu jangan marah dong***, "Don't get angry now!"
kan	asking for confirmation of what was said and equivalent to the tag question, e.g. ***Ini kan bagus warnanya***, "This is a lovely color, isn't it?"

There are also numerous shortened forms, e.g.

gitu	"like that" (cf. *begitu*)
gini	"like this" (cf. *begini*)
kali	"perhaps" (cf. *barangkali*)
gimana	"how? what?" (cf. *bagaimana*)
nih	"this" (cf. *ini*)
tuh	"that" (cf. *itu*)
kalo	"if; that" (introducing a clause) (cf. *kalau; bahwa*)
udah	"already" (past tense) (cf. *sudah*)
aja	"only" (cf. *saja*)

The shortening of words in general is a typical feature of a colloquial, as speakers of English can test for themselves on their own speech. As a result, Jakarta colloquial moves fast, with a minimum of superfluous syllables.

We also find a fondness for foreign words, some Dutch, e.g. *met* ("with") or *snel* ("quick"), and others English, e.g. *so* ("so").

The use of slang is especially prominent in the language of young people, who like to play with the language and create forms that are particularly expressive or humorous. There exist forms that are supposed to be secret, made according to more or less regular patterns. This "argot" is termed *prokem*, and there are little dictionaries of it. Some examples are *doi* meaning "he/she" (*dia*) and also "boy/girlfriend"; *ortu* ("parents", made from *orang tua*); *bokap* "father," and *nyokap* "mother." It is said that there are also in-group slangs for thieves, gays and transvestites, and the inmates of jails.

In general it can be said that the use of non-standard forms stresses intimacy, informality and a heightened level of feeling, in comparison with standard forms. So it is understandable that Jakarta colloquial should be popular among the youth, and that it should have a strong influence on speaking and writing Indonesian in various contexts.

CHAPTER SEVEN

The Writing System

During its long history, Malay has been written in three different scripts, Indian, Arabic and Roman. A script is a system of writing, that is, a set of symbols used to represent sounds. As we saw above, a script derived from India was in use for writing Malay in Srivijaya and in other early Sumatran polities; then, with the adoption of Islam, Perso-Arabic script became the classic means for writing Malay; and the Europeans (in Indonesia, the Dutch) developed their own method for writing Malay, using the common European script, called the Roman alphabet (but called "Latin" letters in Dutch and Indonesian).

Because the writing of Indonesian with Roman characters was a Dutch creation, the original spelling also reflected Dutch spelling conventions. For example, the present sound *u* was spelt *oe*, and this spelling can still be seen in some people's names. The spelling system was reformed in 1972. The changes were not great, but it is useful to be aware of them if one has to read sources from the pre-1972 period.

PRE-1972	POST-1972
j	*y*
dj	*j*
tj	*c*
ch	*kh*

Note that the only digraph left (apart from **ng**), is **kh**, which is a guttural fricative, found only in Arabic loanwords.

The spelling of Indonesian is quite regular—there are very few exceptions to its rules. Indonesian has no tones, and hence no tone markers, and no accents (but see below).

The sounds of Indonesian

Vowels

These are: *a, e, i, o, u*.

a   Always the short sound of "ha!". It is never like English "ay" or the "a" of "cat."

e   Mostly the short sound of the "e" of "open" or "broken" (a mute "e," which linguists call schwa). But in a minority of cases it is different, like the "e" of "egg." The distinction is important, but normally there is no way of telling the difference. However, some dictionaries are helpful enough to use an accent for this second sound, thus *é*, and we do the same in this book.

i   Short and sharp, like the sound in "fit."

o   In closed syllables, like the "o" in "sock"; in open syllables, like the "o" in "go."

u   As in "pull," or the "oo" of "foot," but never the long sound of "food."

It is helpful to divide words into syllables, and to give each syllable its full value, e.g. *ha-us* ("thirsty"), *da-é-rah* ("area").

Consonants

These are as in English, but with the following exceptions:

c   Always as the "ch" in English "child," so never as in "cat."

g   Always hard, as in "gate," so never as in "germ."

h   Always sounded, also in the middle or at the end of a word, e.g. *sudah* ("already"), **Tuhan** ("God").

r   Also always sounded, but not as the American "r"; give it a light roll.

The alphabet

It is also very useful to be able to say the alphabet in Indonesian, as the *names* of the letters (as distinct from their sounds) are different from the English names, and again reflect their Dutch origins. Some are confusing—in spelling your name, for example, it is important to give the right pronunciation for the letters. The following is an approximation:

LETTER	NAME
A	ah
B	bé
C	ché
D	dé
E	é
F	ef
G	gé (hard!)
H	ha
I	ee
J	jé
K	ka
L	el
M	em
N	en
O	oh
P	pé
Q	ki
R	air
S	es
T	té
U	oo
V	fé
W	wé
X	iks
Y	yé
Z	set

Note that the accent used here represents the French *e acute*—a nice, crisp sound, rather than the loose "ay" of English.

The most important letters to watch here are *A* (ah) and *R* ("air"—sound the "r"!), *E* (é) and *I* ("ee," but shorter), because they can get confused; and also the *H* (ha) and *K* (ka).

Some letters, namely *Q*, *V*, *X* and *Z* are very rare in Indonesian, and are found only in loanwords.

CHAPTER EIGHT

What is Indonesian Related to?

Having discovered that Indonesian is a variety of Malay, we can trace what Indonesian is by looking at the position of Malay among its neighboring languages. Just as most European languages are related to each other in various degrees, so too there is the possibility of certain languages in the Asia-Pacific region being related to each other. In this way we can map the place of Malay in Southeast Asia.

Languages are related to each other by being descended from a common ancestor—hence the metaphor of the language family. This kind of "genetic" relationship has nothing to do with the borrowing of words from one language into another. Relatedness is established by means of comparison, and this study, called comparative linguistics, is a highly developed branch of linguistics, alongside descriptive linguistics and sociolinguistics.

Similarities were observed among the languages of Sumatra, those of Madagascar and of islands far out into the Pacific as early as 1783. The family of languages these comprised was first called Malayo-Polynesian, but is today termed Austronesian. According to one estimate, the entire family boasts some 825 different languages, of which 241 are found within the borders of Indonesia. These are separate languages; the term "dialect" should not be used for them, as this refers to geographical differences within one language—dialects are mutually intelligible, whereas separate languages are not.

Austronesian languages are spoken over a very wide area, from Taiwan in the north, southwards through the Philippines and the Indonesian Archipelago, westwards to include Madagascar, and eastwards to include the languages of Melanesia, Micronesia and Polynesia. The languages of Taiwan mentioned are aboriginal languages, and have nothing to do with a form of Chinese. In fact it seems likely that the Austronesian languages were carried from there southwards via prehistoric migrations by sea, beginning perhaps 5,000 years ago, into the Philippines, with one branch then going eastwards, towards New Guinea and thence far out into the Pacific, and another going southwards into Sulawesi and Kalimantan, and from there further into what is now Indonesia. In this way, we can speak of sub-groups within the Austronesian family.

FIGURE 8a: Sub-grouping of Austronesia languages

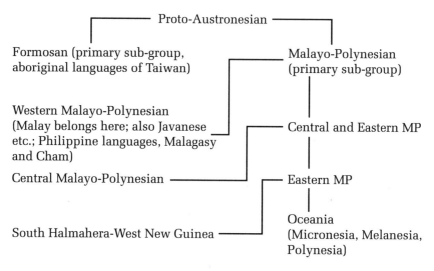

(after Blust 1987)

It will be seen that Malay has its place in the western Malayo-Polynesian sub-group, alongside the other languages of Western and Central Indonesia. Even though Malay is an important member of the group, and is our main interest here, in no sense are the other languages descended from it. So Malay, Javanese, Sundanese, Balinese and so on are all equally members of the Malayo-Polynesian subgroup and descendants of proto-Austronesian. Another misapprehension dating from very early studies is the idea that these languages found their way out of mainland Southeast Asia via the Malay Peninsula; this view is incorrect. It is more likely that members of the family were spread by sea from island to island, as outlined above. Note too that there is no "Indonesian" sub-group as such.

Malay itself probably became established in eastern and southern Sumatra in prehistoric times. It is closely related to certain languages of western Borneo, suggesting that it may well have originated from there. In very early times Malay itself was introduced into parts of western Borneo (including Brunei), southern Borneo, and most importantly, the Malay Peninsula (the present West Malaysia), also including four provinces of what is now southern Thailand: Satun, Yala, Narathiwat and Pattani.

Another way of sketching the position of Malay/Indonesian is to say what it is *not* related to, and this is of interest to those who may have studied other Asian languages. There is no relationship with Chinese, Korean or Japanese; there is also no relationship with Vietnamese, Cambodian or Mon (which belong to the Austroasiatic family), or with Thai and Lao (which belong to the Tai group), or with Burmese (which is a Sino-Tibetan language), or any of the smaller minority languages of the mainland, with one exception. This exception is the Cham language (actually a small group, the Chamic languages), originally found in central Vietnam. Cham is a close relative of Malay, and is thought to have found its way back to the mainland from the area of Borneo in prehistoric times.

Despite what has been said here, there are still a number of curious similarities between items from these languages. For example, compare Malay *ini* with Thai *nii*, both meaning "this"; or Malay *semut* with Thai *mot*, both meaning "ant"; or Javanese *manuk* with Thai *nok*, both meaning "bird."

The overall picture is not quite complete yet. Malay and the other Austronesian languages are not connected with the Australian aboriginal languages, or with the Papuan languages (hundreds of them!) found in the interior of New Guinea, and including a number in eastern Indonesia—in Timor, Alor and Halmahera—which are also non-Austronesian. In the case of some Austronesian languages, there is the possibility of influence from a "substratum" language, that is, one which preceded the Austronesian one, as the Archipelago had certainly been inhabited for thousands of years before Austronesian speakers arrived there.

As an exercise in comparison, I have collected words from eight Austronesian languages (for which dictionaries happened to be available—no other significance!) for 13 items, so that we can take a quick look at the similarities and differences. However, in order to draw valid conclusions, we would need hundreds of items, and in fact a proper comparison should cover more than just vocabulary, and include the sound system and grammar. And the quality of the comparison also depends on the quality of the sources, such as the dictionaries, that are used.

As soon as one starts to collect data, some interesting problems turn up. The items chosen have to be very basic (as here), because as soon as you try to compare verbs, for example "to carry," you are confronted with the question, *which* verb? This is because there are many, used to express the idea of carrying in many different ways. Or there may be a range of words that seem to mean the same thing; one may be everyday, and others used in special contexts, such as ritual or poetry, so which one is going to be chosen for a valid comparison? Even with seemingly simple concepts such as "male" and "female" we have to be on guard, because there could be different terms for human beings and animals. Other items may be specific to some cultures but not others, or have special forms, for example "rice." If you did take "rice," then you would also have to be careful to specify the form: in the field, harvested but not husked, husked, or cooked? There may be different words for each!

Taking a quick look at the table (Table 8a), a few interesting details already emerge. For example, for "person," the form *orang/wong* is restricted to the west, while *tau* is very widespread in the east. For "house" the *rumah/umah* type is very common, but the alternative (*fale, báhay, whare*) is not so strange, as it is connected with Malay *balai*, referring to a certain kind of building. For "three," forms related to *telu* are very widespread, and the Malay *tiga* is the odd form out. Borrowing and historical developments are also complicating factors. For example, Javanese *wadon* is probably taken from Sanskrit *wadhu* ("woman"), and Javanese *srengéngé* ("sun") is derived from *sang hyang wé* ("the holy sun"), found in Old Javanese. Language levels are another problem: should you choose the high or the low form for comparison?

The languages used in the following table are:

- Malay (the basis of Indonesian, an important language of western Indonesia and Malaysia)
- Javanese (found mainly in Central and East Java and the largest regional or ethnic language of Indonesia, with about 100 million speakers)

- Balinese (found on the island of Bali, to the east of Java)
- Sundanese (found in the province of West Java)
- Iban (found in the western part of Kalimantan)
- Samoan (found in Samoa, in the Pacific)
- Tagalog (the largest and most developed of the Philippine languages and the basis of Filipino)
- Maori (the language of the Polynesian inhabitants of New Zealand)

TABLE 8a: Comparison of eight Austronesian languages

ENGLISH	MALAY	JAVANESE	BALINESE	SUNDANESE	IBAN	SAMOAN	TAGALOG	MAORI
person	orang	wong	anak	urang	orang	tagata	táo	tangata
child	anak	anak	panak	anak	anak	tamaitiiti	anák	tamaiti
male	laki-laki	lanang	muani	lalaki	laki	tāne	laláki	taane
female	perempuan	wadon	luh	awéwé	indu'	fafine	babáe	wahine
house	rumah	omah	umah	imah	rumah	fale	báhay	whare
river	sungai	kali	tukad	walungan	sungai	vaitafe	ílog	awa
sun	matahari	srengéngé	matanai	panonpoé	mata ari	ari	lā	raa
moon	bulan	wulan	bulan	bulan	bulan	māsina	buwán	marama
rain	hujan	udan	ujan	hujan	ujan	ua	ulán	ua-ina
water	air	banyu	yeh	cai	ai	vai	túbig	wai
one	satu	siji	besik	hiji	sa	tasi	isá	tahi
two	dua	loro	dua	dua	dua	lua	dalawá	rua
three	tiga	telu	telu	tílu	tiga	tolu	tatló	toru

Examining the words of Indonesian is a fascinating study. We can discover the derivation of some words, find out whether they are shared by related languages, and explore the dimensions of their meaning. This means that they can become our familiar friends, and it certainly helps in remembering them—quite a challenge, when they do not resemble any English or European words at all.

CHAPTER NINE

Loanwords in Indonesian

Many languages contain a large number of words that have been borrowed from others, especially ones spoken by peoples who have been
much in contact with others. English, for instance, contains vast numbers of loanwords from French, Latin, Greek and many other non-Ger-
manic sources, though it is a Germanic language.

Similarly, the majority of words in Malay, and thus also Indonesian, are
Austronesian, while there are others that can be traced back to origins in
other languages. Once borrowed, they of course became part of Malay
and are no longer viewed as "foreign" by speakers of the language. In
many cases, the donor languages belonged to quite different families of
languages, but that makes no difference. The process of borrowing was
part of cultural borrowing in a broader sense, and so runs parallel to the
phases of the long history of the region. Hence one should try to be specific about when the borrowing takes place; and of course the process is
still continuing at this very moment.

The earliest contact with people from outside the region was apparently
with Indian traders, priests and scholars who brought books written in
Sanskrit. These related to Mahayana Buddhism, and were studied in
monasteries located in Srivijaya in southern Sumatra. As early as the 7th
century, words derived from Sanskrit had already entered Malay. The
"Indianized" period of Malay lasted for many centuries, so it is not surprising that quite a number of words were borrowed, but these were by
no means all technical religious terms. It is remarkable that some very
familiar items of vocabulary in modern Indonesian are of Sanskrit origin.

A list of some common Indonesian words deriving from Sanskrit follows, showing the original Sanskrit form and meaning. In some cases
there has been a shift in meaning, scarcely surprising in view of the
length of time involved. In some cases there is a possibility of borrowing
via the intermediary of Old Javanese, and in other cases a Middle Indic
dialect or Prakrit may have been involved, rather than Sanskrit.

INDONESIAN	MEANING	SANSKRIT	MEANING
arti	meaning	*artha*	meaning
atau	or	*athavā*	or
bahasa	language	*bhāṣa*	language
bahaya	danger	*bhaya*	danger
bahwa	that (conj.)	*bhāva*	being, existence
bangsa	nation	*vaṃśa*	lineage, dynasty
béda	difference	*bheda*	separation
benda	object, thing	*bhaṇḍa*	goods, wares
biasa	usual	*abhyāsa*	repeated exercise
bisa	can, able; poison	*viṣa*	poison; effective
biaya	expenses	*vyaya*	loss, expense
cerita	story	*carita*	adventures, story
cuci	wash	*śuci*	pure, clean
guna	use	*guṇa*	(good) quality
harga	price	*argha*	worth, value
harta	property	*artha*	substance, wealth
karena	because	*kāraṇa*	cause
kerja, karya	work	*kārya*	work
mula	beginning	*mūla*	root
nama	name	*nāma*	name
negara	state	*nagara*	town, city
puasa	to fast	*upavāsa*	abstinence
rupa	form, shape	*rūpa*	appearance
saja, sahaja	only; simple	*sahaja*	natural
sama	same	*sama*	equal
saya, sahaya	I; servant	*sahāya*	companion
semua	all	*samūha*	collection
serba	all kinds of	*sarva*	whole, entire
sudah	already	*śuddha*	clear, pure
supaya	so that	*saupaya*	with the aim
tetapi	but	*tathāpi*	even so
upacara	ceremony	*upacāra*	insignia
upaya	effort	*upāya*	means, stratagem

The Islamic religion is of great importance for the Malay and Indonesian-speaking world, and brought with it contact with the wider Islamic community. As we have seen, Islam came to the Indonesian region from India. The holy book of Islam, however, as well as all the Traditions, commentaries and other technical works, were in Arabic. So it is obvious that Arabic is the source of many loanwords in Malay and Indonesian. Alongside it there are a surprising number of Persian loanwords as well, because Persian was the main literary language of Muslim India at that time, and a number of literary works were translated from Persian into Malay when Malay literature was being formed. In some cases, Persian itself borrowed words from Arabic, so that it becomes difficult to say with certainty whether an Arabic loan is direct or via Persian (and this applies in particular to words ending in *-at*). Arabic loanwords in Malay and Indonesian are not related to religion exclusively, but most kinds of scholarship. A brief list provides some examples.

INDONESIAN	MEANING	ARABIC	MEANING
adat	custom	'āda	custom
akhir	end	ākhir	last
akibat	result	'āqĭba	sequel
alam	universe; nature	ālam	world
alamat	address	'alāma	sign
alat	tool	āla	appliances
asal	origin	aşl	origin
asli	original	aşlĭ	original
batin	inner	bāṭin	inner
derajat	degree	daraja	grade
doa	prayer	du'ā'	prayer
dunia	world	dunyā	world
hadiah	gift	hadĭya	gift
hak	right (n.)	haqq	truth
hal	matter, thing	hāl	affair
hasil	yield	hāşĭl	product
hewan	animal	hayawā	living thing
hukum	law	hukm	decree
iklim	climate	iqlĭm	climate
ilmu	science	'ilm	knowledge
jaman	era	zamān	time
jawab	answer	jawāb	answer
kitab	scripture	kitāb	book
kubur	grave (n.)	qubūr	grave
lahir	born	zāhir	outward
maaf	pardon	mu'āf	pardon

mesjid	mosque	*masjid*	mosque
misal	example	*mithāl*	example
miskin	poor	*miskīn*	poverty
mungkin	possible	*mumkin*	possible
murid	pupil	*murīd*	pupil
musim	season	*mausim*	monsoon
perlu	necessary	*fardh*	obligatory
pikir	to think	*fikir*	to think
saat	moment	*sā'a*	period of time
sabar	patient (adj.)	*şābr*	patience
sebab	cause, because	*sabab*	cause, reason
séhat	healthy	*şīhha*	health
selamat	safe	*salāma*	safety
soal	problem	*su'āl*	question
terjemah	to translate	*tarjama*	to translate
umur	age	*'umr*	duration of life
waktu	time	*waqt*	appointed time
yakin	certain	*yaqiñ*	convinced

By comparison, there are not as many loanwords taken directly from Persian. Some are common, but many others are found only in old romantic tales and are now obsolete. Terms often relate to trade or to luxury items. A list follows:

INDONESIAN	MEANING	PERSIAN	MEANING
anggar	to estimate	*angāra*	to estimate
anggur	grape	*angūr*	grape
bandar	port	*bandar*	port
daftar	list	*daftar*	register
destar	head cloth	*dastār*	turban
dewan	council, panel	*dīwān*	department
gandum	wheat	*gandum*	wheat
kawin	married	*kāwīn*	gift for bride
kismis	raisin	*kishmish*	raisin
langgar	chapel	*langar*	shrine
nakhoda	ship's captain	*nā-khudā*	ship's captain
nisan	gravestone	*nishān*	marker
pahlawan	hero	*pahlawān*	leader
pasar	market	*bāzār*	market

saudagar	merchant	*saudāgar*	merchant
takhta	throne	*takht*	seat, throne
tamasya	picnic	*tamāshā*	spectacle, show

The Portuguese loanwords in Malay and Indonesian bring us into perhaps more familiar territory, at least for those who know European languages (so a gloss need not be included). This may help when one is attempting to learn new vocabulary. In general, the terms taken from Portuguese apply to objects that were new, or not yet known in that form, in the Malay-speaking world, at the time when the Portuguese came into contact with the local population. The Portuguese language became a lingua franca in some places, and a mixed (Christian) population arose, so that Portuguese words easily found their way into Malay. Some of these were, however, restricted to particular areas and are now obsolete, while others entered the mainstream and are still familiar today. A list follows:

INDONESIAN	MEANING	PORTUGUESE
bangku	bench	*banco*
bendéra	flag	*bandeira*
bonéka	doll	*boneca*
gardu	guardhouse	*guarda*
garpu	fork	*garfo*
geréja	church	*igreja*
jendéla	window	*janela*
kartu	card	*carta*
kéju	cheese	*queijo*
keméja	shirt	*camisa*
keréta	carriage, cart	*carreta*
kutang	brassiere	*cotão*
lélang	auction	*leilão* ("sale")
lemari	cupboard	*armário*
mandor	overseer	*mandador*
méja	table	*mesa*
mentéga	butter	*manteiga*
meski (pun)	although	*mas que*
minggu	week, Sunday	*Domingo*
Natal	Christmas	*Natal*
palsu	fake	*falso*

Paskah	Easter	*Páscoa*
peluru	bullet	*pelouro*
péna	pen	*pena*
peniti	pin	*alfinete*
perséro	(business) partner	*parceiro*
pésta	party, feast	*festa*
perangko	stamp	*franco ("postage paid")*
pita	ribbon	*fita*
roda	wheel	*roda*
ronda	night watch	*ronda*
sabun	soap	*sabão*
saku	pocket	*saco ("bag")*
sekolah	school	*escola*
sepatu	shoe	*sapato*
serdadu	soldier	*soldado*
témpo	time	*tempo*
ténda	tent	*tenda*
terigu	wheat	*trigo*
tinta	ink	*tinta*

Chinese have traveled to Indonesia for centuries, sometimes for trade but also to settle, with the result that a number of loanwords from Chinese are to be found in Malay and Indonesian. So these are worth studying too. It has to be borne in mind that the term "Chinese," however, is far from precise, as there are many different Chinese languages, and it is most unlikely that the loanwords we are concerned with should be traceable to Mandarin. Instead, it is logical to seek their origin precisely where the majority of immigrants themselves originated.

A revealing study by Russell Jones has shown that we have to look to the coastal area of southern China. About 90% of the loanwords in Malay/Indonesian derive from the Hokkien (also known as Minnan or Southern Min) language, which itself consists of many dialects. The source of borrowing turns out to be the southern Hokkien dialect of the area around Amoy (Xiamen) in southern Fujian Province.

Some of the Chinese loanwords are of very limited use, and are found only in the Indonesian-Chinese community, while others are quite familiar. A glance at the list seems to show that the majority of these words relate to either food or business. Here are a few examples (without attempting to indicate the original Hokkien form):

INDONESIAN	MEANING
anglo	brazier
bakmi	noodles with pork
bécak	pedicab
cat	paint
ébi	dried shrimps
gua, gué	I (informal only)
gudang	warehouse
jung	junk, boat
kécap	soy sauce
kongsi	company, association
kué(h)	cake
kuli	manual laborer
lici (léci)	litchi
loteng	second floor of a building
lu	you (informal only)
lumpia	spring roll
mi	noodles
nyonya	lady; Mrs
pit	brush (pen)
sampan	boat
tahu	bean curd
taogé (taugé)	bean sprouts
tauké	employer
téh	tea
tukang	craftsman
ubin	floor tile

There are literally hundreds of loanwords from Dutch in modern Indonesian. The majority of these entered the language in the first half of the 20th century (although there are a few much older ones), and the process seems to have continued for long after Independence and to mark an enduring pattern. The Dutch loanwords are by no means restricted to the official, business or technical spheres, but cover a wide range of domains. Some examples from the domestic area are (showing the original Dutch):

INDONESIAN	MEANING	DUTCH
setom	dryclean(ing)	*stomen*
setrika	(to) iron	*strijken*
stoplés	stoppered glass jar	*stopfles*
setrik	hair ribbon	*strik*
setéker	electrical plug	*stekker*
seprai	bedspread	*sprei*

The parts of a bicycle include:

ban	tyre	*band*
pélek	rim (of wheel)	*velg*
péntil	valve	*ventiel*
sadel	seat	*zadel*
setang	bar	*stang*

A few items relating to the office:

kantor	office	*kantoor*
bloknot	note pad	*bloknoot*
potlot	pencil	*potlood*
setip	eraser	*stuf*
pulpén	fountain pen	*vulpen*
dorslah	carbon copy	*doorslag*
kwitansi	receipt	*kwitantie*
formulir	form	*formulier*

Some amusing examples:

indehoy	to have a romp (sexually)	*in de hooi* ("in the hay," but the correct Dutch would be *in het hooi*!)
béha	bra	*BH, bustehouder* ("bustholder")
bestik	steaks (also chicken)	*biefstuk* ("steak")
strongking	pressure lamp	*Stormking* (a brand name)

More importantly, in modern Indonesian we find a large number of words with an ending **-asi** or **-isasi**. This is a productive process. The ending corresponds to English "-ization," but is in fact from Dutch -atie or -isatie. A few random examples:

antisipasi	anticipation	*anticipatie*
indoktrinasi	indoctrination	*indoctrinatie*
informasi	information	*informatie*
inovasi	innovation	*innovatie*
invéstasi	investment	*investatie*
koordinasi	coordination	*coördinatie*
réputasi	reputation	*reputatie*
sosialisasi	socialization	*socialisatie*

Similarly, the Indonesian ending **-si** reflects the Dutch -tie or -sie rather than English "-ion." For example:

produksi	production	*productie*
profési	profession	*professie*
rédaksi	editorial staff	*redactie*
solusi	solution	*solutie*

Other similar forms from Dutch, not English, are for example:

insidén	incident	*incident*
instrumén	instrument	*instrument*
pasién	patient (n.)	*patient*
prosédur	procedure	*proceduur*

However, the adjectival ending **-il** (Dutch -eel) has now been replaced with **-al** (English "-al"), e.g.:

kontroversial	controversial	*controversieel*
proporsional	proportional	*proportioneel*

And some confusing words:

polis	policy (insurance), not "police"	*polis*
répétisi	rehearsal, not repetition	*repetitie*

There exist a surprising number of expressions in Indonesian that turn out to be loan translations from Dutch, as we find if we compare the two, thus explaining why some words look a little odd from an English viewpoint. Here are some examples:

angkatan	generation, class	*lichting* ("lifting")
batu	battery	*vuursteen* ("fire-stone, flint")
jajak pendapat	opinion poll	*opiniepeiling* ("fathoming of opinions")
jam bicara	consulting hours	*spreekuur* ("talking hour")
kapal selam	submarine	*duikboot* ("dive boat")
keberatan	objection	*bezwaar* ("weigh down")
lemari és	refrigerator	*ijskast* ("ice cupboard")
mengemudi	to drive (car)	*(be)sturen* ("to steer")
negara bagian	state	*deelstaat* ("part-state")
pengisap debu	vacuum cleaner	*stofzuiger* ("dust-sucker")
pesawat terbang	aircraft	*vliegtuig* ("flying machine")
rumah sakit	hospital	*ziekenhuis* ("house of the sick")
sekolah dasar	primary school	*basisschool* ("basic school")
tandatangan	signature	*handtekening* ("hand marking")
tempat	seat (on bus, plane)	*zitplaats* ("sitting place")
tenaga	staff member	*(werk)kracht* ("working strength")
ulangan	test (in school)	*herhaling* ("repetition")
undang-undang dasar	constitution	*grondwet* ("basic law")

The number of borrowings from Dutch is to be explained by the presence of a large Dutch population in the Netherlands East Indies and their predominant position in colonial society, associated with the high prestige of all things European, as well as the fact that the Indonesian elite were fluent in Dutch, and some had even been to The Netherlands for further study. The Dutch language was the window on the modern world, as other European languages were not widely known.

Indonesian words that can definitely be traced to English are less common. This contrasts with the situation in Malaysian Malay (see above).

There seem to be two areas where English words are borrowed. The first is the informal or "pop" sphere. Sometimes the loanwords from English show a shift in meaning in comparison with the original, or a transfer to a different category, suggesting that the knowledge of English is not deep. A few examples are:

baskét	basketball
béking	backing
buking	booking, to book
droping	additional budget
flu	influenza, flu
geng	gang
hit	very popular
hot	very sexy
rilis	to release (song, product)
stress	stressed

The second area where borrowings from English take place is the technical area, bringing us right up to date. Sometimes a new Indonesian term has been formed on the basis of English, and sometimes it happens that an English word is inserted into a text in an unassimilated form, so that this cannot be called a real loanword, although it may soon become one. Many new terms are needed for developing fields such as finance and banking, science and technology. Some examples from information technology are given under language development in Chapter 4.

A reading of modern prose reveals that the main source of enrichment in the Indonesian language is Javanese. These words have generally been taken in their original form and meaning, and apparently fulfil an expressive need in the language. Some random examples are:

bakal	will, going to
bocah	kid
jéngkél	annoyed
ketimbang	compared with
lumrah	normal, common
manut	obedient, docile
mirip	to resemble
pamor	shine, luster

paro	half
pasok (me-)	to supply
rembuk (me- -kan)	to discuss, confer about
tembang	song
wadah	container, umbrella organization

Apart from these, there are many terms that seem to be "concocted" Javanese forms, in the sense that they have been made up of Javanese elements in order to create a new term, although we do not know when or by whom. For example:

rékayasa (me- -kan)	to engineer, organize, fix
wawancara (me- -i)	to interview

The development of terminology has been mentioned in Chapter 4.

Finally, a fertile source of borrowing in Indonesian is the Jakarta dialect, which has its own forms that are not normally accepted as standard Indonesian, but nevertheless are valued for their informal expressive impact. Some examples are:

denger	to hear
mémblé	lousy
muter	to play (a tape)
narik	to drive (car, bus)
nangkering	to sit up high, perch
ngetop	to go to the top
péngén	to want to

The Jakarta colloquial has been discussed in Chapter 6.

CHAPTER TEN

The Indonesian Word

Somebody beginning on the study of Indonesian will obviously be curious to find out "what it is like," that is, what its words look like and how they are strung together to make meaningful utterances or texts. The claim has sometimes been made that Indonesian is "easy," and while it is true that one can achieve satisfying results within a reasonable time, it is also a fact that there are a number of unfamiliar features, and quite a bit of effort is needed to understand, remember and apply these correctly. From the viewpoint of a speaker of English, some seemingly normal elements are missing, whereas Indonesian has some interesting ways of saying things that English does not have.

Language is not chaos, otherwise we would not be able to understand each other. There are accepted conventions or regularities—consensus on what conveys what meaning. But it would be wrong to expect hard and fast rules, because an exception generally seems to turn up. Indonesian has rules and exceptions too, although it may be more regular than English. Students have to master the rules and remember the exceptions if they are going to produce acceptable and comprehensible Indonesian. Speech or writing that ignores the rules just runs the risk of sounding silly, even if we can still guess the meaning.

We can make a start by introducing the concept of word-formation. Some words have no special marks, while others show changes in form in different places. For example in the English *constitute, constitutes, constituted, constituting* we can see a word without an ending, one with the ending "-s," one with "-d," and one with "-ing." Parallel with a change in the form of the word goes a change in its meaning. So the principle that applies is: a different form gives a different meaning. And this is valid for Indonesian too.

In some Indonesian words an element can be observed at the front of the word (this is termed a prefix), or at the end of a word (a suffix), or a combination of both. And of course there are plenty of words that are used without any addition at all; we can call these simple or underived forms.

Words can be classified into groups, categories or parts of speech, on the basis of what kind of work they do and what position they occupy in a sentence (the sentence will be discussed in the next chapter).

The Noun

A noun is a word that refers to a thing (including a person or an abstraction); it is the "name" of a thing. It can be simple or derived.

Examples of simple nouns:

perang	war
tentara	army
senjata	weapon

Examples of derived nouns:
1. These nouns have a prefix *ke-* and a suffix *-an*; together they are combined with an adjective and form an abstract noun (like English words with "-ness").

kegagalan	failure
kemenangan	victory
kekalahan	defeat

2. These nouns have a prefix *pe-* followed by a nasal sound (which varies, see below), and means "the person who does…" cf. English "-er"/"-or."

pemimpin	leader
penasihat	advisor
pengemudi	driver

3. These nouns also have a prefix *pe-* with a nasal sound, but have the suffix *-an* as well. They mean "the act of…" (cf. English words with "-ing" [e.g. selling, treating, releasing] and many other forms):

penjualan	sale
pengobatan	treatment
pembébasan	release

4. These nouns have a prefix **per-** and a suffix **-an** and indicate "affairs/matters relating to…"

peralatan	equipment
perkamusan	lexicography
perékonomian	economics

5. These nouns have a suffix **-an**, and indicate generally "the result of… (the action of the corresponding verb)."

sasaran	target
anggaran	budget
tuduhan	accusation

Nouns such as these do several kinds of work in a sentence: they can be the subject of a verb, the object of the action of a transitive verb, or they can qualify or be qualified by another noun, in a possessive relation.

Possession is indicated merely by means of word order (no suffix, preposition or postposition). The principle is this: the possessor follows the thing possessed, e.g. **anggaran negara** "national budget" (i.e. the **anggaran** of the **negara**).

Nouns do not need to have an article (definite or indefinite), like the English "the" and "a." The Indonesian noun is basically indefinite ("a"), but is made definite ("the") by the use of some qualifying word, such as a demonstrative or possessive word. An English translation has to supply an article appropriate to the context.

In English, many nouns have "-s" to indicate the plural. Indonesian, however, does not do this. In fact, there is no change at all, so with any noun we have the option of translating with either the singular or the plural, depending on what fits. However, there is a process often mentioned here, namely doubling or reduplication, e.g. from **pohon** "tree," we get **pohon-pohon** "trees." But we have to be careful here: **pohon-**

pohon is certainly plural, but there is an added element of meaning, that is, generality, "trees (in general)." Further, doubling never occurs when a numeral is used—because plurality is already clear.

The Pronoun

Indonesian has a set of pronouns that can be arranged according to "person" (first, second and third), including singular and plural, and the degree of formality. The latter is important, because using the right pronoun affects the relations between people ("me" and "you"). The following table shows how this works:

TABLE 10a: Pronouns

	ENGLISH	NON-FORMAL	NEUTRAL	FORMAL
First person	I	*aku*	*saya*	*saya*
	we (inclusive)	*kita*	*kita*	*kita*
	we (exclusive)	*kami*	*kami*	*kami*
Second person	you	*kamu*	*anda*	*saudara*
		engkau		*anda*
	you (plural)	*kalian*	*kalian*	*kalian*
Third person	he, she (it)	*dia*	*dia*	*beliau*
	they	*meréka*	*meréka*	*meréka*

It is obvious that this system has features that English lacks. For example, there are two pronouns for "we"; the term "inclusive" means "we, plus you (all of us)," while the term "exclusive" means "we, not including you (just us)." So the difference can be important. For example, **anak kita** ("our child") means the child that is both mine and yours!

For the purposes of conversation, the beginning student need only remember **saya, kita** and **kami, anda, dia** and **meréka.**

The English word "it" is an interesting case. For example, it is often part of an impersonal expression ("It is raining"), and does not require a translation into Indonesian (**hujan** means both "rain" and "to rain," so "it is raining" is simply **hujan**). "It" and "they" are also often replaced by the noun to which they refer, so that we use the noun rather than a pronoun. The pronoun **meréka** is used only for people. **Dia** is used for both "he" and "she"—gender is irrelevant.

There are no changes in form corresponding to the English "I/me," "we/us," "he/him," and "she/her" for subject and object forms. For the possessive, as usual the possessor follows the thing possessed, e.g.

> **rumah saya**   my house
> **rumah kami**   our house
> **rumah meréka**   their house

In the case of **dia**, though, this pronoun is generally replaced by a suffix **-nya**, e.g. **rumahnya**, his/her house. By the way, this suffix has several other functions as well, one of which is worth mentioning here, namely a vague demonstrative meaning, translated with "the," e.g. **cuacanya** ("the weather"), or replacing "your" in order to be more indirect or polite, e.g. **alamatnya** ("your address").

There are two more cases where a suffix replaces the pronoun to express possession, and these are: **-ku** for **aku**, and **-mu** for **kamu**, e.g. **adikku** ("my younger brother/sister") or **kakakmu** ("your elder brother/sister"). But note that both **aku** and **kamu** (and hence also **-ku** and **-mu**) stand in the non-formal column, and in other words are only used in situations of closeness, as with friends you know well.

The pronoun "you" is probably the most difficult to render in Indonesian. Apart from **kamu**, **anda** is safe, while **saudara** sounds rather cold and formal. In practice, though, people very often do not use a real pronoun but a substitute, either a kinship term or the name of the person being addressed. Among the so-called kinship terms, **Bapak** (literally "father") and **Ibu** (literally "mother") are the commonest. They are respectful, and are applied to a gentleman and a lady respectively, just to say "you."

The Adjective

Adjectives tell us something about a noun, specifying some quality it has. In Indonesian the adjective always follows the noun it qualifies (in contrast to English), e.g. **rumah mahal** ("expensive house"). It never changes its form (as it does in French or German) to agree with its noun in any way.

Some useful adjectives are:

mudah	easy
sukar	hard
mahal	expensive
murah	cheap
tinggi	high, tall
rendah	low
besar	big
kecil	small
muda	young
tua	old

We make the comparative ("more," "-er") with the word *lebih*, and the superlative ("most," "-est") with *paling*, both placed in front of their adjective, e.g. *lebih besar* ("bigger"), *paling tua* ("oldest").

The Numeral

The numeral system of Indonesian is very simple and regular. The numbers one to ten are:

1	*satu*
2	*dua*
3	*tiga*
4	*empat*
5	*lima*
6	*enam*
7	*tujuh*
8	*delapan*
9	*sembilan*
10	*sepuluh*

The "-teens" are characterized by *-belas*:

11	*sebelas*
12	*duabelas*
13	*tigabelas*
14	*empatbelas*
15	*limabelas*

16	*enambelas*
17	*tujuhbelas*
18	*delapanbelas*
19	*sembilanbelas*

And the multiples of ten feature *puluh* (N.B. *sepuluh* = one *puluh*):

20	*dua puluh*
30	*tiga puluh*
40	*empat puluh*
50	*lima puluh*
60	*enam puluh*
70	*tujuh puluh*
80	*delapan puluh*
90	*sembilan puluh*

The hundreds feature *ratus*:

100	*seratus*
200	*dua ratus* and so on

The thousands feature *ribu*:

1.000	*seribu*	("1,000")
2.000	*dua ribu*	("2,000") and so on

Further, we have:

10.000	*sepuluh ribu*	("10,000")
100.000	*seratus ribu*	("100,000") and so on

The millions feature *juta*:

1.000.000	*sejuta*	("1,000,000")
2.000.000	*dua juta*	("2,000,000") and so on

And one billion is *satu milyar*.

Note that in Indonesian the decimal point is shown by a comma, and a dot is used to separate thousands from the hundreds and so on.

Fractions are made using the prefix *per-* attached to a numeral. For example, "quarter" is *perempat*, so "one quarter" is *seperempat* and "three quarters" is *tiga perempat*. The prefix *se-* seen in *sepuluh* and other numerals means "one," but it also has the meaning of "whole" or "same" in other contexts.

The Verb

The verb is undoubtedly the most important and most complex part of Indonesian. The student will need to take account of such terms as "transitive" and "intransitive," as well as "active" and "passive," as will be outlined below.

Some verbs are simple, while others are formed by derivation. Some examples of common simple verbs are:

keluar	to go out
masuk	to go in
pergi	to go
datang	to come
pulang	to go home
tidur	to sleep
bangun	to wake, get up

Note how sometimes one word covers what is expressed by more than one word in English. These verbs are all intransitive. This means that they never have an object.

Another group of verbs that are intransitive have the prefix *ber-*. These sometimes refer to an action, e.g.

berjalan	to go, travel
berkunjung	to visit (followed by "to")
bertemu	to meet (followed by "with")

or mean "to have" something, e.g.

  berpendapat literally "to have the opinion," to be of the opinion
  berumur   "to have the age," to be aged (so many years)
  bernama   "to have the name," to be named (X)

But the majority of Indonesian verbs have the prefix ***meN-*** (where ***N*** stands for a nasal sound which varies, depending on the initial letter of the base-word). Most of these verbs are transitive; that is, they can have an object. Seeing that the process of nasalization is so important, we should present it in detail by means of a table, followed by some examples.

TABLE 10b: Nasalization of verbs

INITIAL LETTER OF THE BASE-WORD	FORM OF THE PREFIX *meN-*
any vowel, ***h, g, kh***	*meng-*
r, l, y, w	*me-*
m, n, ny, ng	*me-*
k	*me-*, *ng* replaces ***k***
p	*me-*, *m* replaces ***p***
s	*me-*, *ny* replaces ***s***
t	*me-*, *n* replaces ***t***
d, c, j, z	*men-*
b, f, v	*mem-*

Examples, showing base-word and ***meN-*** form:

INITIAL LETTER	BASE-WORD: *meN-*	MEANING
(any vowel)	*ambil: mengambil*	to take
h	*hadap: menghadap*	to face, front on
g	*ganggu: mengganggu*	to disturb, bother
r	*rasa: merasa*	to feel, sense
l	*lamar: melamar*	to apply, propose
m	*muat: memuat*	to hold, carry, contain
n	*nikah: menikah*	to marry
k	*kirim: mengirim*	to send
p	*panggil: memanggil*	to call, summon
s	*sambut: menyambut*	to welcome, receive
t	*tulis: menulis*	to write
d	*dapat: mendapat*	to get, obtain

c	*catat: mencatat*	to note
j	*jawab: menjawab*	to answer, reply
b	*bawa: membawa*	to carry, bring.

This table enables one to find the base-word of a verb. This is important because words are listed under the base-word, not the **meN-** form, in most dictionaries, as this makes it possible to see the whole range of derived forms under one head. There are, however, a few cases of ambiguity, where you may have to look in two places in order to find the word.

The forms with **meN-** are always active. Because they have an object they can also have a passive form. The difference is this. In the active, we have the sequence: subject, verb with **meN-**, and object (not counting other information, such as adverbs or phrases of place and so on). But in the passive, a crucial change takes place. What was the object becomes the subject and moves to the front of the sentence, the verb changes its form (loses its **meN-**), and what was the subject becomes the "agent" and has to be accommodated as well. Note that the passive is very common in Indonesian, and serves to focus attention on the thing or person being acted on, rather than the thing or person who does the action.

Here is a summary of passive verbal forms, with literal translation, showing the position and form of the agent:

saya baca	read by me
kamu (or other word for "you") *baca*	read by you
dibacanya (or sometimes *dia baca*)	read by him/her
kita/kami baca	read by us
meréka baca	read by them

The form **dibaca** ("read") is very important, as it is passive but does not specify the agent, that is, who did the reading, so a noun agent can then be introduced after the verb with the word **oléh** ("by"), e.g. **Buku itu sudah dibaca oléh banyak orang**, "That book has been read by many people."

A large number of Indonesian verbs can be observed to have a suffix, either **-kan** or **-i**, with the prefix **meN-** or a passive form. These verbs are transitive. It is hard to predict exactly when these suffixes occur or to define the aspect of meaning they add. For example, verbs with **-kan** often have a "causative" meaning, but not always. Some examples:

- from **kembali** ("to come back"), we have **mengembalikan** ("to bring/send back")
- from **jatuh** ("to fall"), we have **menjatuhkan** ("to drop")
- from **naik** ("to go up, rise"), we have **menaikkan** ("to raise")

Verbs with the suffix **-i** sometimes have a "locative" meaning, in that the action is directed to a place or thing, e.g.

- from **air** ("water"), we get **mengairi** ("to irrigate" ["to apply water"])
- from **obat** ("medicine"), we get **mengobati** ("to treat" ["to apply medicine"])

However, please remember that there are a number of other interesting meanings that cannot be listed here. Further, one is not free to construct one's own verbal forms—they already exist, as found in the dictionary or not. The kind of analysis that students carry out is merely to assist in identifying meanings and understanding structures.

There is another interesting verbal prefix, **ter-**, which can roughly be termed "passive," in that it often translates with a passive. It can tell us about a state, for example:

terletak	located
tertulis	written (not oral)
terkenal	well known
tersebut	aforementioned
tertanggal	dated (e.g. a letter)
terlibat	involved
tertarik	interested
terhormat	respected

or about an accidental or inadvertent action (one which usually has no agent), for example:

terjadi	to happen
terkejut	to be startled

teringat	to recall, remember
terasa	to feel (have a sensation; N.B. base-word *rasa*)
tertawa	to laugh
tersenyum	to smile
terbuat	made (not known by whom)
tertelan	swallowed by accident
tertidur	to fall asleep

Some More Interesting Verb Forms

As mentioned earlier, Indonesian is sometimes able to say things with one word that English cannot, and it would be useful to draw attention to a few of these here to illustrate the point.

There is a group of intransitive verbs (that is, without object), marked by a prefix *ber-* and a suffix *-an*, with several different meanings, and thus belonging to different categories.

One of these meanings is "reciprocity," that is, an action done "to each other." Some examples will make this clear:

berciuman	to kiss each other

sometimes with a doubled base-word, e.g.

berpelukan-pelukan	to hug each other

In some cases a word is added to complete the meaning (but this is not an object), e.g.

berpegangan tangan	to hold hands (each other's, of course, so we don't need to write that)
bertukaran cincin	to exchange rings (as a token of engagement)

There are a number of common words that belong here and which the student should know, referring to a mutual relationship or spatial positioning, e.g.

berkenalan	to be acquainted
berpacaran	to be boyfriend and girlfriend
bersangkutan	to be concerned, involved

berhubungan	to be connected, related
berdekatan	to be near (each other)
bertentangan	to be opposite (each other)
berdampingan	to be alongside (each other)
berhadapan	to be facing (each other)
berbatasan	to border on

Words such as these take the preposition **dengan** "with," to introduce the person or thing with which we have the relation.

There are other, less common ways, in which reciprocity is expressed, namely with a type of reduplication, e.g.

tawar-menawar	to bargain, haggle with each other

and using the word **saling**, e.g.

saling mencintai	to love each other

A second category also featuring **ber-** and **-an**, but completely separate from the above, is the "random action" verbs. These have a multiple subject and suggest that the action occurs in a random or confused way, e.g.

bersérakan	to be scattered, littered about (e.g. the papers on my desk)
beterbangan	(note the form **be-** here for **ber-**) to fly up in all directions (e.g. a flock of birds when chased by a child)
berkeliaran	to roam, cruise, wander about (e.g. taxis looking for a fare)

There are also some interesting intransitive verbs with the prefix **ber-** and a suffix **-kan**, meaning "to have something as"; these need a complement, to follow and complete the meaning. Some examples:

berdasarkan	to be based on.... (e.g. the State on the *Pancasila*)
berasaskan	to be founded on the principle of...
bersumberkan	to have as source...
berisikan	to have as contents...

The above is merely a sample; there are many more aspects of Indonesian verbs that the student will want to explore, in the process of becoming better acquainted with the language.

Modal Words

These could also be called auxiliary verbs. They are placed immediately before the verb, and serve to express useful things, such as tense:

akan	will, going to (future)
sedang	is/are .... -ing (present continuous)
sudah/telah	has/have ... -ed (past or perfect tense)

or ability and necessity:

bisa/dapat	can, able to
sempat	to have the opportunity to
harus	should, ought to, to have to
perlu	must, to need to

Adverbs

There are all sorts of adverbs, for example adverbs of time (saying "when"):

sekarang	now
nanti	soon, shortly
tadi	just now, a little while ago

or adverbs of frequency (saying "how often"):

kadang-kadang	sometimes
jarang	seldom, rarely
selalu	always
sering	often

or adverbs of manner (saying "how"):

pelan-pelan	slowly

or using **dengan** before an adjective, for example:

> **dengan tepat**   exactly

or using **secara**, for example:

> **secara terbuka**   openly, in an open way.

Adverbs are generally placed either at the beginning or the end of a sentence.

Prepositions

These little words are placed in front of a noun or pronoun, to form a phrase that is found at the beginning or at the end of a sentence. Please note that in Indonesian (as in other languages) the use of prepositions is highly idiomatic, so literal translations from English are often incorrect. The main prepositions are:

di	in, at, on (mainly spatial)
ke	to (spatial only)
dari	from
dengan	with
tanpa	without
dalam	in, within
akan/terhadap	towards, regarding

The spatial prepositions are combined with words of place to form phrases indicating location, if necessary followed by a noun in a possessive relation, for example:

> **di luar**   outside
> **di luar kota**   outside town

Other place words are:

dalam	the inside	**di dalam**	inside
atas	the top	**di atas**	on top (of), above
bawah	the bottom	**di bawah**	under, below

Similarly with **ke** and **dari**. Other important place words are:

sini	here, this place
situ	there, that place
sana	over there (out of sight),

so we get:

di sini	here (in this place)
ke sini	here (to this place)
dari sini	from here,

and so on with **situ** and **sana**.

CHAPTER ELEVEN

The Indonesian Sentence

When thinking about how words are arranged in an Indonesian sentence, the distinction between subject and predicate may be useful. The subject is the thing or person being talked about, and the predicate is what is being said about that.

Normally we expect to find the subject first, followed by the predicate. The principle is that what comes first gets most attention. So if the order is reversed, this means that extra emphasis is being placed on the word or words of the predicate. But it may be hard to express this in a translation. For example:

Aku bingung.   I'm confused.
Bingung aku!   I've no idea what to do!

The first is a mere statement of fact, whereas the second is a cry from the heart.

The subject could be a noun, pronoun or a word-group equivalent to a noun. But the predicate could be a noun, an adjective, or a verb.

1. If we have a sentence composed of noun or pronoun plus noun, then the latter explains what the subject is, in a sort of equation, A = B, e.g.

Beliau penerbit.   He is a publisher.

This is a complete sentence. It does not contain a word equivalent to the English "is," but this does have to be added in the translation to make good English. If the sentence is long or complicated, though, then the break between subject and predicate can be hard to detect, and so there is a word that is used to occupy the slot of "is," namely *adalah*. This never changes its form for tense, person and so on (unlike English "is," "are," "was," "were"). For example:

Satu di antaranya adalah akadémi seni yang berlokasi di Jalan Pejaten Raya.
One of them is the art academy located on Pejaten Raya Road.

Here it would be confusing to omit the word **adalah**.

2. An adjective can also be a complete predicate in itself, e.g.

Dia capai.   She is tired.

In such a case, the adjective in fact looks like a verb, "to be tired," because "is/are/was/were" is contained within it.

The other use of adjectives, alluded to above, as qualifying words is quite different. **Perjalanan panjang** ("a long trip") is not a sentence. But it would be if we added something, such as **itu** ("that"): **Perjalanan itu panjang.** ("That trip was long.").

In this case the separation of subject and predicate becomes clear.

3. The majority of predicates consist of a verb of some kind, or contain a verb together with varying amounts of other information. The verb may be intransitive; in that case, it has no object, but may be followed by something else, e.g.:

Dapur terletak di belakang rumah.
The kitchen is located at the back of the house.

Or the verb may be transitive, and if it has an object, that object will follow it directly, followed in turn by other information, if needed, e.g.:

Polisi menangkap kawanan pencuri kemarin malam.
The police arrested the gang of thieves yesterday evening.

But if the verb is passive, there is no object, though there is of course a subject, e.g.:

Hasil curian terbesar diperoléhnya dari kediaman Susan.
Literally "The biggest loot was obtained by him from the residence of
Susan." i.e. "He got the biggest loot from Susan's residence." (It is
often best to translate the Indonesian passive into an English active.)

There is another way to add extra information to the simple sentence,
that is, by attaching a clause introduced by the relative pronoun *yang*,
which we can translate as "who," "which," or "that," directly following
and qualifying a noun. For example:

*Dérétan rumah makan di Kampung Alor, yang kini dikenal dengan
sebutan "Kampung Indonésia," setiap hari dipadati petugas PBB.*
The row of eating houses in Kampung Alor, which is now better
known by the name "Indonesian Kampung," is crowded with UN offi-
cers every day.

Sebagian dolar yang diperoléhnya juga ia kirim ke kampung.
Part of the dollars he gets he also sends home to the village.

Or a clause can explain "why," introduced by a word such as *karena*, e.g.:

Bisnisnya ternyata makin maju karena kurang pesaing.
His business turned out to do better and better because there was a
lack of competitors.

Or again, verbs of telling, thinking and so on can be followed by *bahwa*
("that"), introducing a clause which contains the content of the speech,
though etc. And similarly verbs of asking, wondering and so on are followed by *apakah* ("whether," "if"), introducing the content of the question and so forth.

If it is necessary to make a condition, then we can use a clause introduced by *kalau* ("if"), or *asal* ("provided"). And if we need to make a
concession, we can use a clause introduced by *meskipun* or *walaupun*
("although").

Apart from statements such as the sentences outlined above, it is of
course also important to be able to make requests and to ask questions.

Requests

It is in fact rare to give a bare order, because we have to bear in mind the hearer's feelings—that is, if we want a positive response! And thus there exist various ways of formulating one's wishes, using helpful introductory words or final particles, e.g.:

> *Minta yang manis saja, ya!*
> Just give me the sweet ones, okay? (Literally "I ask for only the sweet ones, yes."

Minta actually means "to ask for," and a more formal verb with the same meaning is *mohon*, e.g.:

> *Mohon balasan dalam témpo seminggu.*
> Kindly give me a reply within a week.

> *Tolong dipindahkan ke kamar depan.*
> Please shift it to the front room.

Here *tolong* suggests "do it for me." The use of a passive verb with *di-* makes the request less personal or more indirect.

The use of *ya* softens the request ("okay?"), and sentences such as these can be made politer by also using a term of address, such as *Pak* or *Bu*, just to show that we acknowledge the addressee's status, although in English is would be unusual to add "Sir" or "Madam."

The word *harap* is often found as a polite, rather formal imperative, e.g.:

> *Tamu harap lapor.* Visitors must report.
> *Harap tenang pada jam tidur.* Kindly be quiet at rest times.

The opposite to a request is a prohibition. Indonesian has one word for the English "don't/do not," namely *jangan*. Interestingly, this can also be used with a passive verb, e.g.:

Piring-piring itu jangan ditaruh di lantai.
Don't put those plates on the floor. (Literally "Don't let the plates be placed on the floor." This use of the passive is because the focus is on what should or should not happen to the plates, not on who does the action.)

Questions

Any statement can be turned into a question simply by placing the word *apakah* in front of it (or *apa* in informal speech), e.g.:

Pembantu kami berasal dari Jawa Tengah.
Our domestic helper comes from Central Java.

Apakah pembantu kami berasal dari Jawa Tengah?
Does our domestic helper come from Central Java?

Note that there is no inversion (reversing the order of subject and verb) to make a question, or use of an auxiliary verb ("do/does"), as in English. The only case where inversion is seen is in a sentence beginning: *Boléh saya...* ("May I...?"), which may in fact betray the influence of Dutch *Mag ik...* ("May I...?").

Otherwise, questions are formed with the use of an interrogative word, as follows.

Apa? ("what?")
> *Apa namanya?* What do you call it? (What is its name?)
> *Beli apa, Pak?* What do you want to buy?
> Note that the word order is quite different; in the Indonesian, *apa* is the object of the verb *beli* ("buy"), and so cannot occupy the initial position.

Mana has two meanings:
> 1) where, which place?
> *Anda tinggal di mana?* Where do you live? (Literally "You live where?")

2) which (one out of several)?

Hotél mana yang dipilih? Which hotel did you choose? (Literally "Which hotel was chosen?")

Note that *yang* and a passive are needed after *mana* in this sentence, despite the fact that the English "choose" may look like an active form.

Berapa ("how many?" "how much?")

This word is very useful when out shopping. We can say:

Berapa harganya? How much does it cost? (Literally "How much is its price?")

Berapa jam kalau terbang ke Menado? How many hours does it take to fly to Menado?

But if the word order is reversed, we get a different meaning:

Jam berapa? What time is it?

And similarly:

Tanggal berapa? What date?

Tahun berapa? Which year?

Bagaimana ("how?" "in what way?" "like what?")

Bagaimana rasanya? What does it taste like?

Bagaimana maksudnya? What do you mean? (Literally "What is the intention?")

Bagaimana caranya? How do you do it? (Literally "What is the method?")

Mengapa ("why?" "for what reason?")

Mengapa jam keberangkatan kita ditunda begini? Why has our time of departure been postponed like this?

Kamu kelihatan pucat. Mengapa? You're looking pale. Why is this?

Kapan ("when?")

Kapan ada keréta api ke Surabaya? When is there a train to Surabaya?

This can only be used in questions; if "when" can be replaced with "if," it is *kalau*. And if it can be replaced with "at the time," it is *pada waktu* or *ketika*.

Siapa ("who?")

> ***Siapa memesan nasi goréng ini?*** Who ordered this fried rice?
> ***Siapa nama saudara?*** What is your name? (Literally "Who is...?")
> ***Gedung ini milik siapa?*** To whom does this building belong? (Literally "This building is the property of whom?")

CHAPTER TWELVE

Journalistic Prose

Without doubt the best manifestation of modern Indonesian is to be found in what we may call "journalistic prose." This is written by an able army of men and women and published in magazines such as *Tempo* and *Gatra*. The same sort of language is found in newspapers and in an oral form in TV news bulletins, although perhaps less varied and less interesting.

The journals alluded to deal with current affairs in a broad sense, and in fact contain a wide range of items in 130 pages, such as lifestyle, entertainment, science and technology, information technology, crime, health, overseas news, interviews and so on. This means that the student seeking the latest news and opinions on what is happening in Indonesia cannot avoid the need to read and analyze this type of Indonesian writing.

Writers are capable of composing highly effective pieces, sometimes quite critical of the establishment, that succeed in making a point. In order to appreciate this, it pays to read right through to the end, as a close reading reveals attention to structure, and the sting is often in the tail. A regular feature is a back page devoted to an essay (**esai**), which may well be regarded as a literary form.

The style can be described as crisp and racy, a style that does not hesitate to use neologisms or borrow a word from the colloquial if needed to make a point. It is this that makes such magazines a prominent source of information for those interested in how the Indonesian language is changing. The items are normally carefully edited and contain few typographical errors (in contrast to what used to happen in the past).

Considering some of the marks of journalistic prose, there are a number of words that seem to be typical of the style, and contrast with more ordinary, everyday Indonesian. Here are some examples, with a more down-to-earth equivalent and English translation:

"JOURNALISTIC" INDONESIAN	EVERYDAY INDONESIAN	ENGLISH
acap	*sering*	often
belakangan	*baru-baru ini*	recently
buntutnya	*akhirnya*	finally, in the end
gara-gara	*oléh karena*	because of
ikut	*juga*	also
kala	*waktu*	when
kendati	*walaupun*	although
ketimbang	*daripada*	than
lantaran	*oléh karena*	because of
pekan	*minggu*	week
saking	*oleh karéna*	because of
sembari	*sambil*	while
silam	*yang lalu*	ago
tengah	*sedang*	in the process of
tutur	*kata*	to say
ujar	*kata*	to say
usai	*habis*	over, finished

It is interesting that **bahwa** ("that") is not used after verbs of saying and so on. This seems to be intended to make the prose flow faster, and may even be regarded as a sign of the influence of English style.

As we also see in newspapers, in headings verbs lose their prefix **meN-**, e.g. **Goyang Inul Goyang Iman** ("Inul's Sway Sways Faith"), where the second **goyang** should be understood as **menggoyang** ("to rock, sway").

Occasionally the drive to find a sophisticated or technical modern term leads to excesses, such as the term **primordialitas**, which looks like "primordiality," but means "primitive condition," or **semaksimal mungkin**, "as maximally as possible", that is, simply, "as much as possible".

We find a liking for a method of opening a sentence with a single word followed by a comma, then the rest of the sentence, for example:

Uniknya, ...	The unique thing (feature) is, ...
Ironisnya, ...	The ironic thing is, ...
Sayangnya, ...	Unfortunately, ...
Biasanya, ...	Normally, ...

From the viewpoint of structure, these can be considered as complete "nominal" sentences of the A = B type. In the same way, we find indications of time or reason:

Selama ini, ...	Till now, ...
Mulai Februari ini, ...	Since last February, ...
Maka, ...	And so, ...
Sebab, ...	This is because...
Karena itu, ...	For that reason...
Mulanya, ...	Initially...
Alhasil, ...	As a result, ...

Some authors like to liven up their prose with the use of sayings, such as:

Pagar makan tanaman, literally "The fence eats the crop," that is, the one who should be protecting people in fact exploits them.

Nasi sudah jadi kerak, literally "The steamed rice has turned to crust," that is, it's too late to do anything about it.

Mana ada makanan siang yang gratis, which is a direct translation of the English "There's no such thing as a free lunch."

Bagaimana mau membersihkan rumah dengan sapu yang sudah kotor? "How do you expect to clean the house with a dirty broom?"

Anjing menggonggong kafilah tetap berlalu, literally "The dogs bark but the caravan keeps on going." Nothing stops you if you are determined.

It has often been remarked that Indonesian is very fond of acronyms and initialisms, but English and Dutch also have them. In Indonesian they are formed with initials or with parts of words, and are sometimes familiar and other times quite difficult to decipher. They refer to a range of institutions, organizations and concepts. The reader of journalistic prose should have access to a dictionary of acronyms. Here are a few examples:

APBD   **Anggaran Pendapatan dan Belanja Negara**
National Budget

Bappenas   **Badan Perancang Pembangunan Nasional**
National Planning Board

Bulog   **Biro Logistik**
Logistics Bureau

BUMN   **Badan Usaha Milik Negara**
State Owned Enterprise

DKI Jakarta   **Daerah Khusus Ibukota Jakarta**
Special Capital Area of Jakarta

DPRD   **Dewan Perwakilan Rakyat Daerah**
Regional Peoples' Representative Council

Golkar   **Golongan Karya**
(name of a functional political grouping)

Inprés   **Instruksi Présidén**
Presidential Instruction

Jabar   **Jawa Barat**
West Java (and the names of many other provinces)

Mendagri   **Menteri Dalam Negeri**
Minister of Internal Affairs (and similarly with other ministers)

PDIP   **Partai Demokrasi Indonesia – Perjuangan**
(name of a political party)

Pemilu   **Pemilihan Umum**
General Election

Pémprov	**Pemerintah Provinsi** provincial government
Polri	**Polisi Républik Indonesia** Police of the Republic of Indonesia
Puskésmas	**Pusat Keséhatan Masyarakat** Community Health Center
SD	**Sekolah Dasar** Elementary/Primary School
SMU	**Sekolah Menengah Umum** General High School
SMA	**Sekolah Menengah Atas** Senior High School
TNI	**Tentara Nasional Indonesia** Indonesian National Armed Forces
UU	**Undang-undang** law/act/ordinance

Here are some examples of contemporary prose.

From *Gatra* February 15, 2003, page 34:

ANAK TANGGA KE PLANET MERAH

Misi ruang angkasa mencatat sejumlah sukses. Dari penemuan semikonduktor baru hingga perbaikan teleskop di angkasa. Juga penangkapan satelit yang kesasar.

Tak ada kata mundur dalam kamus Lembaga Antariksa dan Penerbangan Amerika Serikat (NASA). Hanya 21 bulan setelah Apollo 1 terbakar pada 1967, NASA berhasil mengirim Apollo 11 ke bulan. Waktu untuk pulih setelah ledakan Challenger awal 1986 juga tak sampai tiga tahun. Meledaknya pesawat ulang-alik Columbia, 1 Februari lalu, juga dipastikan tak akan membuat langkah NASA surut dalam mengeksplorasi [the original has *mengeplorasi*] *angkasa luar.*

Memang seperti dikhayalkan Johannes Kepler, pada abad ke-17, tentang perahu-perahu angkasa yang menggunakan angin matahari untuk menyeberangi angkasa menuju Mars, ribuan misi ke angkasa luar telah dilakukan manusia. Anak-anak perahu yang diangankan Kepler adalah astronot-astronot modern saat ini. Dalam misi ruang angkasa itu, tak sedikit astronot menjadi korban.

Lepas dari soal bahaya itu, misi angkasa Amerika Serikat dengan pesawat ulang-aliknya menorehkan sejumlah prestasi. Endeavour, misalnya, pada 4 Desember 1993 sukses memperbaiki teleskop Hubble, yang mengalami 'rabun dekat'. Teleskop angkasa luar raksasa itu menempati orbitnya 587 kilometer di atas permukaan laut, setelah diantar Discovery, 29 April 1990. Ternyata, lensanya mengalami kesalahan konstruksi, bergeser sepersekian milimeter. Citra yang dihasilkan kurang sempurna.

NASA pun kecewa. Untuk merampungkan teleskop yang terpasang pada konstruksi logam campuran sepanjang 20 meter itu, NASA melibatkan 10.000 ahli, dan menelan biaya US$2 milyar atau Rp 20 trilyun. Ahli NASA melatih astronotnya bergerak di dalam air, untuk latihan melakukan perbaikan di angkasa luar. Tingkat kesulitannya sangat tinggi. Ibarat memakai sarong tangan bisbol untuk memperbaiki arloji.

The following is a moderately literal translation:

LADDER TO THE RED PLANET

Space missions have listed a number of successes. From the discovery of a new semiconductor to repairing a telescope in space. Also the capture of a runaway satellite.

The word "retreat" does not exist in the dictionary of the National Aeronautics and Space Administration (NASA). Only 21 months after Apollo 1 was burnt up in 1967, NASA succeeded in sending Apollo 11 to the moon. The time needed to recover after the explosion of Challenger at the beginning of 1986 was not even three years. The explosion of the Columbia shuttle on 1 February last is also destined not to make NASA step back from exploring space.

Just as Johannes Kepler imagined in the 17th century with regard to space ships using sun winds to cross space to Mars, men have made thousands of missions into space. The crew that Kepler was thinking of are the modern astronauts of today. In these space missions not a few astronauts have lost their lives.

Apart from the question of danger, United States space missions with the shuttle have chalked up a number of achievements. Endeavour, for example, on December 4, 1993 succeeded in repairing the Hubble telescope, which was suffering from "myopia." This giant space telescope occupied its orbit 587 kilometers above the surface of the sea after it was taken there by Discovery on April 29, 1990. It turned out that its lens was suffering from a construction fault and had shifted so many millimeters. The image it provided was not quite perfect.

NASA was disappointed. To complete the telescope attached to an alloy construction 20 meters long, NASA involved 10,000 experts and used funds of US$2 billion or 20 trillion rupiah. NASA experts trained their astronauts to move in water as practice for carrying out repairs in space. The level of difficulty was very high, comparable to wearing baseball gloves to repair a watch.

From *Gatra* February 22, 2003, page 22A:

GOYANG BOR MENUJU PEMILU

Semula hanya dari panggung kecil di kampung, Inul meroket jadi selebriti nasional. Dari ribuan rupiah, kini honornya ratusan juta rupiah. Berlian pun betengger di giginya.

Anak kampung di kota Pasuruan, Jawa Timur, Ainul Rokhimah, pernah punya mimpi cukup aneh. Ia naik balon udara bersama Megawati Soekarnoputri, membubung menembus awan. Jauh di bawah, ayah Mega, Soekarno, melambaikan tangan. Sang proklamator seakan melepas kepergian balon itu. Sayang, mimpi itu tidak tuntas. Inul Daratista, begitu Ainul

Rohkimah kini punya nama komersial, keburu terjaga. Inul menangis.

Dara berusia 24 tahun ini tak mengerti apa makna mimpi itu. Tak lama kemudian namanya ramai dibicarakan. Ia dikenal sebagai pesohor tingkat nasional. Namun, bayangan untuk bersua dengan keluarga Soekarno tak pernah pupus.

Angan-angan itu menjadi nyata, Senin pekan lalu. Sore itu, ia tampil bersama Taufiq Kiemas, suami Presiden Megawati. Inul dan Taufiq menjadi bintang tamu "Waroeng Toedjoe", acara ngobrol serius-santai yang digelar televisi swasta TV 7. Usai acara, Inul didaulat menyanyi, sambil memperagakan goyangannya, yang bergerak ala bor, dari atas ke bawah.

Taufiq ikut berjoget. Bahkan, ia "bermurah hati" memeluk Inul. Taufiq tampaknya kesengsem pada Inul. "Inul ini dimasukkan jadwal kampanye, yah! Goyangnya bagus. Nggak ada yang aneh, kok! Yang namanya dangdut memang harus seperti ini," kata Taufiq, seperti dituturkan kembali oleh Inul kepada GATRA. Taufiq sendiri mengakui, gerakan Inul memang boleh. "Anak itu punya talenta, harus disyukuri," katanya. Jorokkah goyang molennya Inul? "Tidak. Coba lihat, kakinya menutup rapat, nggak ada yang mengangkang," katanya.

Translation:

'DRILL' GYRATION HEADS FOR ELECTION

Originally from only a small stage in the village, Inul has rocketed to become a national celebrity. From thousands of rupiah, now her fee is hundreds of millions of rupiah. Even diamonds perch on her teeth.

A village girl from the town of Pasuruan, East Java, Ainul Rokhimah once had quite a strange dream. She was going up in a balloon with Megawati Soekarnoputri, soaring through the clouds. Far below, Mega's father, Soekarno, was waving. The Proclaimer seemed to be seeing the balloon off. Unfortunately, the dream wasn't finished. Inul Daratista—such is Ainul Rokhimah's commercial name now—woke up in a hurry. Inul cried.

The 24-year-old maiden didn't know what the dream meant. Not long after that her name was much talked about. She was known as a famous figure at national level. Even so, the idea of meeting Soekarno's family never faded.

The idea turned to reality on Monday of last week. That afternoon she appeared with Taufiq Kiemas, President Megawati's husband. Inul and Taufiq were guest stars on "Waroeng Toedjoe," the serious-relaxed talk show presented by independent station TV 7. After the program, Inul was persuaded to sing while showing off her gyration which moves in the manner of a drill, from top to bottom.

Taufiq joined in dancing. He was even "generous enough" to hug Inul. Taufiq looked as if he was fascinated with Inul. "I'm going to put Inul here onto the campaign timetable, right! Her swing is great. There's nothing queer about it! After all it's *dangdut*, it has to be like this," said Taufiq, as Inul reported back to GATRA. Taufiq himself admitted that Inul's movements are okay. "This girl has talents—we should be grateful for them," he said. Are Inul's cement mixer-like movements obscene? "No. Just take a look, her legs are closed tight, they're never wide apart," he said.

From *Gatra* February 22, 2003, pages 96–97:

RANCAGE DARI SAKURA

Lima belas tahun tanpa putus.
Mengalirkan sastra daerah yang mandek.

SUGIARTA SRIWIBAWA:
LEBIH MANTEP PAKAI BAHASA JAWA

Lewat mesin tik tua, pria sepuh ini masih terus mengalirkan imajinasinya. "Anak saya melarang mengetik di depan komputer," kata Sugiarta Sriwibawa, 71 tahun, kepada GATRA. Dengan peranti kuno itu ia menyelesaikan Candhikala Kapuranta, novel berbahasa Jawa, dalam waktu dua bulan. Karyanya ini kemudian diterbitkan Pustaka Jaya. Pekan lalu, Candhikala Kapuranta – secara harfiah berarti "senjakala yang memancarkan merah kekuningan" – meraih Hadiah Sastra Rancage untuk karya sastra Jawa terbaik 2003.

Ajip Rosidi, Ketua Dewan Pembina Yayasan Rancage, menyebut Candhikala *karya dengan alur yang dinamis dan unik. Keunikan ini, menurut Ajip, dibangun oleh kekuatan pengarang menggarap latar budaya Jawa. Ia bercerita tentang Munah, gadis "ndeso" yang terlempar ke kehidupan priayi Solo setelah jadi selir Raden Mas Puspawicitra. Dengan setting perkawinan lintas kelas ini, pusat cerita berpindah-pindah: antara dunia pri- ayi dengan tatanan rumit dan* wong cilik *yang spontan.*

Menurut Sugiarta, awalnya novel ini ditulis dalam bahasa Indonesia. *Tapi terhenti pada halaman ketiga. "Lebih* mantep *pakai bahasa Jawa," kata Sugiarta, kelahiran Solo, Jawa Ten- gah, 31 Maret 1932. Padahal, Sugiarta bukanlah orang baru di dunia tulis-menulis. Sejak 1951, ia dikenal sebagai penyair – dalam bahasa Indonesia tentu. Karya-karyanya dimuat dalam, antara lain,* Mimbar Indonesia, Siasat, Zenith, Seni, Kisah, *dan* Budaya Jaya – *penerbitan presisius masa itu.*

Dia juga pernah tercatat sebagai wartawan Antara *dan* Sinar Harapan, *lalu sebagai redaktur penerbitan Pustaka Jaya sampai 1998. Kini, dia bekerja di bagian penerbitan Universi- tas Indonesia. Selain* Candhikala, *sudah terbit kumpulan puisinya,* Garis Putih. *Ia juga menerjemahkan karya sastra penulis asing, misalnya Junichiro Tanizaki dan Kahlil Gibran, serta menulis beberapa biografi. "Hadiah Rancage ini bentuk rangsangan buat penulis lain berkarya," kata Sugiarta.*

Selain Sugiarta, Rancage juga diberikan kepada lima sas- trawan lain (lihat: Lima Pemenang Rancage). Mereka masing- masing mendapat Rp 5 juta. Ketika Rancage dimulai, pada 1989, hadiah hanya diberikan untuk sastra Sunda. Barulah pada 1994, kategorinya diperluas dengan Jawa, disusul sastra Bali pada 1998. "Masih mungkin diperluas ke wilayah lain," kata Ajip Rosidi, dengan syarat harus sudah dibukukan.

Menurut Ajip, Rancage memang berhasil merangsang perkembangan sastra Sunda, Jawa, dan Bali. Lihatlah penerbi- tan buku sastra di tiga daerah itu. Pada 2002, buku bacaan Sunda mencapai 27 judul, lebih dari dua kali lipat terbitan tahun sebelumnya, yang cuma 13 judul. Penerbitan karya sas- tra Jawa pada 2002 berjumlah 10 judul, tahun sebelumnya hanya tujuh judul. Begitu pun Bali: delapan judul pada 2002, dari hanya dua judul tahun sebelumnya.

Penilaian Ajip didukung I Made Sangra, pakar sastra Bali yang meraih Hadiah Rancage 1998. "Daya dorongnya hebat terhadap pengembangan sastra Bali modern," katanya. Pengakuan yang sama diberikan Rachmat Taifik Hidayat, Direktur PT Kiblat Utama, yang khusus menerbitkan buku Sunda. Ia merasa, Rancagelah yang mengerek Kiblat Utama, yang baru berdiri pada Oktober 2000. Sudah dua tahun berturut-turut buku terbitannya menyabet penghargaan. "Pembaca sangat antusias," kata Taufik kepada Ida Farida dari GATRA.

Tapi, para pengusung sastra Jawa justru menganggap Rancage tak ada apa-apanya. Agus Winarno, pemilik penerbit CV Bintang menyebutkan, penerbitan buku sastra Jawa sampai sekarang tetap seret. "Karena tak laku, tak ada yang berminat menerbitkan," kata Agus kepada Rachmat Hidayat dari GATRA. Baiklah. Namun, bagaimanapun, ada yang patut dipuji dari Rancage: kesinambungan. Sejak pertama diberikan, pada 1989, Rancage tak pernah absen memberi penghargaan.

"Belum ada hadiah sastra yang mampu bertahan lebih dari lima tahun," kata Ajip, yang April ini akan kembali ke Indonesia setelah hampir 22 tahun jadi pengajar mata kuliah studi Indonesia di Osaka University, Jepang. Untuk sastra Indonesia, memang ada penghargaan seperti Khatulistiwa Award dan Hadiah Sastra Lontar. Tapi, usianya masih muda: kini baru menginjak tahun ketiga. Untuk sastra daerah, Rancage melenggang sendiri.

Penjurian sastra Jawa tahun ini dipercayakan pada Sri Widiati Pradopo dari Lembaga Bahasa Yogyakarta. Sastra Bali dinilai oleh Dharma Putra, pakar sastra Bali modern dari Universitas Udayana, Denpasar. Untuk sastra Sunda, siapa lagi kalau bukan Kang Ajip sendiri. Sebanyak 27 buku sastra Sunda (termasuk bacaan anak-anak) yang terbit sepanjang 2002 dikirim ke meja Ajip di Osaka. Di "negeri sakura" inilah penulis asal Jatiwangi, Jawa Barat, itu menyimak, memilah, dan memilih karya yang berhak memboyong hadiah.

Ajip juga tak segan-segan merogoh sakunya untuk melanggengkan Rancage. Setelah Yayasan Rancage berdiri pada 1993, urusan pendanaan sejatinya menjadi tugas yayasan. Namun, prakteknya, masih saja uang pribadi Ajip jadi andalan. Sumbangan yang masuk tak cukup untuk menalangi biaya penyelenggaraan acara, honor para juri, dan hadiahnya sendiri.

Hidayat Tantan,
Bambang Sulistyo, dan
Irwan Andri Atmanto

A fairly close English translation follows:

RANCAGE FROM THE CHERRY BLOSSOMS

Fifteen years unbroken
Promoting the stalled flow of regional literatures

Sugiarta Sriwibawa:
More confident using Javanese

By means of his old typewriter this elderly gentleman is still promoting the flow of his imagination. "My children forbid me to type at the computer," Sugiarta Sriwibawa, aged 71, told GATRA. With that old machine he completed *Candhikala Kapuranta*, a novel in Javanese, within two months. This work of his was then published by Pustaka Jaya. Last week, *Candhikala Kapuranta*—which literally means "the dusk that spreads a yellowish red glow"—won the Rancage Prize for Literature for the best work of Javanese literature in 2003.

Ajip Rosidi, Chairman of the Steering Committee of the Rancage Foundation, called *Candhikala* a work with a dynamic and unique plot. This unique quality, according to Ajip, is created by the author's strength in treating the Javanese cultural background. He tells about Munah, a "rustic" girl who is thrown into the life of the Solo gentry as a minor wife of Raden Mas Puspawicitra[1]. With this setting[2] of a marriage across class lines, the focus of the story moves back and forth between the world of the gentry with its complicated structure and the spontaneous "little people."

Sugiarta said that he began writing this novel in Indonesian, but got stuck on page three. "I felt more confident writing in Javanese," said Sugiarta, who was born in Solo, Central Java, on March 31, 1932. But in fact Sugiarta is no stranger to the world of writing. He has been recognized as a poet since 1951—in Indonesian, of course. Amongst others, his works were included in *Mimbar Indonesia, Siasat, Zenith, Seni, Kisah* and *Budaya Jaya*, the prestigious publications of that era.

He has also been noted as a journalist with *Antara* and *Sinar Harapan*, and then as an editor with the publisher Pustaka Jaya up to 1998. At present he works in the publishing section of the University of Indonesia. As well as *Candhikala*, a collection of his poems, *Garis Putih*, has appeared. He also translates works by foreign authors, such as Junichiro Tanizaki and Kahlil Gibran, and has written several biographies. "This Rancage Prize is a form of stimulus for other authors to produce works," said Sugiarta.

Besides Sugiarta, Rancage was also given to five other literary figures (see: *Five Winners of the Rancage*[3]). They each got five million rupiah. When the Rancage began, in 1989, the prize was only given for Sundanese literature, and only in 1994 were the categories extended to include Javanese, and Balinese literature in 1998. "It's still possible to expand into other regions," said Ajip Rosidi, on condition that they should have appeared in book form.

In Ajip's opinion, the Rancage has indeed succeeded in stimulating Sundanese, Javanese and Balinese literature. Consider the publishing figures for books from these three areas. In 2002 books for reading in Sundanese reached a total of 27 volumes, more than twice the number for the year before, when only 13 appeared. A total of 10 works of Javanese literature appeared in 2002, and the year before only seven. Similarly with Bali, where eight appeared in 2002, compared with only two the year before.

Ajip's assessment is supported by I Made Sangra, an expert on Balinese literature who won the Rancage Prize in 1998. "It has been a terrific incentive for the development of modern Balinese literature," he said. The same claim was made by Rachmat Taufik Hidayat, Director of PT Kiblat Utama, which specializes in publishing books in Sundanese. He thinks it is Rancage that has lifted Kiblat Utama, which was only set up in October 2000. For two years in succession its books have carried off the award. "The readers are very enthusiastic," Taufik told Ida Farida from GATRA.

However, the bearers of Javanese literature don't regard the Rancage as having anything special. Agus Winarno, who owns the publisher CV Bintang, declared that the publication of Javanese literature is still sluggish. "Because there's no demand, no one is interested in publishing it," Agus told Rachmat Hidayat from GATRA. Okay. Nevertheless, in any case, the Rancage can be praised for something, that is, its continuity. Since it was first given in 1989, it has never failed to give an award.

"There has never been a literary prize that was capable of lasting more than five years," said Ajip, who is going to return to Indonesia this April, after almost 22 years as a teacher of Indonesian studies at Osaka University in Japan. For literature in Indonesian there are of course awards such as the Khatulistiwa Award and the Lontar Prize for Literature, but they are still young—now just entering on their third year. For regional literatures, the Rancage stands alone.

This year the judging for Javanese was entrusted to Sri Widiati Pradopo from the Language Institute of Yogyakarta. Balinese literature was assessed by Dharma Putra, an expert on modern Balinese literature from Udayana University in Denpasar. And for Sundanese literature, who other than dear old Ajip himself. No fewer than 27 books of Sundanese literature (including readers for children) that appeared in the course of 2002 were sent to Ajip's desk in Osaka. There in "cherry blossom country" this writer, born in Jatiwangi, West Java, examined, sorted and selected the works that deserved to carry off the prize.

Ajip has also not hesitated to reach into his own pocket in order to preserve the Rancage. After the Rancage Foundation was set up in 1993, the business of funding has actually been the task of the foundation, but in practice it still relies on Ajip's private money. The contributions received are not enough to cover the cost of organizing events, paying honoraria for judges and the prizes themselves.

Hidayat Tantan,
Bambang Sulistyo, and
Irwan Andri Atmanto

[1] The original spelling, *Purpawicitra*, has been corrected from the novel.

[2] This is the word in the original, using an English term; "theme" might have been better.

[3] This refers to an item that appeared at the foot of the same pages, but is not reproduced here.

CHAPTER THIRTEEN

A Literary Dimension

Those who begin on the study of Indonesian will probably already be aware of its value and usefulness for conversation with Indonesians and for reading all sorts of sources containing information on the current affairs of the country. But they may not yet realize that this language (and we include Malay here, not just its form as Indonesian) has been used for the purposes of creative literature for some centuries. In this sense it can stand alongside some of the other languages of Southeast Asia.

It is quite likely that literary works were created in Malay in the Buddhist period (say, 7th–13th centuries), but actual examples dateable to this period are lacking. Possibly writers used Sanskrit at this time, and there was certainly a disruption when the Chola king of South India invaded the Malay area in 1025.

However that may be, it was the rising influence of Islam in the Malay world that led to the creation of a literature of considerable sophistication in Malay, partly inspired by models in Arabic and Persian, and partly of indigenous origins. The hundreds of extant works in Malay (termed Classical or Traditional Malay, in contrast to Modern) are contained in manuscripts written with ink on paper and using Arabic script. The works comprise both prose and poetry. The prose works include **kitab**, technical books on Islamic theology and law, and also **hikayat**, long narratives of a romantic or epic nature, telling of the adventures of heroes (some Islamic and some not), as well as **sejarah**, historical works on the origins and development of various Malay sultanates. In poetry, the main genre is the **syair**. Even though we are talking about a written literature here, the oral dimension is part and parcel of it, as works were mostly intended to be read aloud, that is, appreciated and perceived by ear, rather than merely by eye. As a result they display features such as fulsomeness and repetition that are essential when reciting to an audience. Furthermore, poetical works such as **syair** were intended to be sung to particular melodies or chants.

This "Islamic" Malay literature arose as early as the 14th century, flourished from the 15th to the 18th century, and declined after that. Nevertheless, to a certain extent it can still be regarded as the heritage of Malay-speaking (or Muslim) communities in West Malaysia, Brunei, and some parts of western Indonesia such as Riau.

The growing presence of Europeans, mainly the Dutch and the British, from the late 18th century onwards, can be considered as instrumental in change in Malay, in that local writers came into contact with Europeans and began to write about the things they saw about them, often in the form of the travelogue. In this way there arose works which can be called "transitional." Examples are the writings of Munsyi Abdullah, the *Hikayat Abdullah* (completed in 1843) and *Kisah Pelayaran Abdullah* (about his voyage to Kelantan in 1838), which present his experiences and ideas in an individual and realistic style. Another good example is Ahmad Rijalludin's *Hikayat Perintah Negeri Benggala*, describing the author's visit to Calcutta in 1810.

Later in the 19th and early 20th century a different stream contributed to Malay literature. This employed what was called Low Malay, and the authors were often from the Chinese community resident in Batavia. The language they used was the common one for communication between Chinese, "natives" and Europeans at that time. Sometimes they described crimes as reported in the press, and sometimes they translated Chinese classics such as *The Three Kingdoms*. Such books appeared in instalments in roman characters. The best known figure in this field is Lie Kim Hok (1853–1912), who even published a grammar of Batavian Malay (1884). An example of the kind of story produced is *Tambahsia, Soewatoe tjerita jang betoel soedah kedjadian di Betawi, Antara Tahoen 1851–1856* (*Tambahsia, a tale that really happened in Batavia between 1851 and 1856*), third printing 1914, published by the company N.V. Hap Sing Kongsie in Gang Pinggir, Semarang.

Here is a small sample in the original spelling (from pages 198–9 at the end of the story):

Sa'at itoe Tambahsia soedah terajoen di atas tiang penggantoe-ngan, tetapi algodjo itoe tida berlakoe bengis teken tali gantoe-

ngan, hanja di biarken sadja, sampei lama'an baroe Tambah-
sia brenti kekedjoetan dan habis djiwanja, setelah Toewan
Dokter soedah priksa djikaloek betoel Tambahsia telah mati,
baroe majidnja di toeroenken dari atas gantoengan, lantas di
masoeken dalem peti mati, dan teroes terkoeboerken di tanah
Sentiong Tandjoeng dengen di iringken bebrapa orang politie.

At that time Tambahsia was already swinging on the gallows, but the executioner did not act cruelly toward him by tightening the rope but just left him alone, until at last Tambahsia stopped twitching and his life was gone. After the Doctor had examined him and found that he was really dead, then his body was taken down from the gallows, put in a coffin, and directly buried in the Chinese Cemetery at Tanjung, escorted by several policemen.

Such stories give a fascinating picture of the mixed society of the Indies, in this case depicting the mid 19th century. This is by no means a "high" literature, but it did bring Malay literature down to earth from the classics, spread the habit of reading, and prepared the ground for a further development of literature.

This came in the early decades of the 20th century, but it cannot be called a direct continuation of what went before. This new movement arose from quite a different social and cultural source, namely the growing class of people who had been educated in Dutch and thus became acquainted with the Dutch literature of the late 19th century. In particular it was writers of Minangkabau (West Sumatran) origin who became inspired to write in Malay. The Minangkabau language is closely related to Malay, and Minangkabau prizes the good use of language.

With the spread of elementary education from 1907 there was a need for reading materials, and this need was filled by a government office, the Bureau for Popular Literature, which became the Balai Pustaka in 1917 and in the next decades published large numbers of titles in Malay, Javanese and Sundanese. Some of the editors for Malay came from the teaching profession, and they included Sutan Takdir Alisjahbana (already mentioned previously).

Quite a number of Western novels were translated, and these were probably of considerable influence in the development of novel writing in Malay. The new works display the marks of individualism and realism and so can be regarded as the beginnings of Indonesian literature. The first original novel was ***Azab dan Sengsara*** by Merari Siregar, published in 1921, followed by ***Sitti Nurbaya*** written by Marah Rusli in 1922. These and the later Sumatran authors wrote moralizing stories that centered on the theme of conflict between the desire for individual freedom, in particular in the choice of marriage partner, and the restrictive pressure of Minangkabau custom (***adat***). The language of the novels, which were published by **Balai Pustaka**, was edited by Nur Sutan Iskandar, who, like many of his colleagues, had passed through the teachers' training collage at Fort de Kock (now Bukittinggi, West Sumatra), and was probably the most influential figure in this period. His works have been described as possessing a "really remarkable suggestive power."

Just as the Japanese Occupation (1942–45) freed the Indonesian language to assume its new role as national language, the events of the period 1945–49, called the Revolution, freed Indonesian writers and provided them with a powerful source of inspiration. The Indonesian nation was struggling for freedom and recognition, and those days of conflict and suffering leading to the birth of the nation find echoes in literary production, in both prose and poetry, that is simple and direct, echoing down the coming years.

But the 1950s were a time of political confusion and growing economic chaos, so that by the early 1960s there was little opportunity for literary work of any value, and the only trend was that of "socialist realism." Following the convulsions of 1965–66, and the opening of the New Order, a range of new voices were heard, originating from various regions, sometimes from less privileged backgrounds, and giving expression to social concerns in the form of, for example, short stories. The literature of the post-New Order ***reformasi*** period and beyond is a story still to be told.

Probably the most durable figure in post-war Indonesian literature, at least in the estimation of outside observers, is Pramoedya Ananta Toer (1925–), the author of a large number of prose works covering a period from 1947 up to 1988, most of them translated into English and Dutch.

There was a long gap in his production from 1965 to 1980, due to his detention on the island of Buru as a communist sympathizer. Five major novels appeared in the period 1980–88, namely **Bumi Manusia** (*This Earth of Mankind*, 1980), **Anak Semua Bangsa** (*Child of All Nations*, 1980), **Jejak Langkah** (*Footsteps*, 1985), **Gadis Pantai** (*The Girl from the Coast*, 1987), and **Rumah Kaca** (*House of Glass*, 1988). These works have a historical theme, in contrast to earlier ones, which are often of an autobiographical nature, as for example **Bukan Pasarmalam** (*No Night Fair*, 1951), which tells about the death of the narrator's father during the Revolution. Here is an extract in translation (pages 99–100):

> The Chinese man said:
> "Yes, why do we have to die alone? To be born alone too? And why do we have to live in a world full of human beings? And if we have been able to love someone, and that person loves us too..." He knelt down and peeped through the window into the inner room where the body was lying alone. He went on, "Like our late friend, for example—why do we then have to part in death? Alone, alone, alone. And another one is born. Another one, another one. Why aren't people born in a crowd and die in a crowd? I'd like this world to be like a night fair."
> The three friends laughed at what the Chinese said. And the Chinese himself laughed. Other people didn't understand what he said. And he didn't understand it himself. Then the discussion ceased.

Indonesian has also been used for poetry, as well as prose. This poetry is free verse, with little reference to traditional forms, and likewise it is highly personal. A number of prominent figures have produced work and some of this may be of lasting value. However, it should be borne in mind that the readership is very small (the same could be said for poetry in many Western countries!), and precisely because of its private nature, sometimes to the point of obscurity, it is not likely to appeal to many. One well-known poet, a Javanese academic from Solo, once commented that in order to express himself adequately he would have to write in Javanese, thus underlining the fact that Indonesian is essentially a second language for most people, and therefore does not possess the expressive power of a mother tongue.

A curious example that seems to illustrate this point is the long poem **Pengakuan Pariyem** by Linus Suryadi AG published in 1981. This was widely read and recited at the time, and was appreciated both for its content and its hypnotic rhythms. But its special feature is the use of a high proportion of words of Javanese origin and many references to Javanese culture, localized in Yogyakarta, which gave it a deep resonance with its audience. Here is a sample (pages 124–5):

"Ya, ya, Pariyem saya
Maria Magdalena Pariyem lengkapnya
'Iyem' panggilan sehari-hari
dari Wonosari Gunung Kidul
Sebagai babu nDoro Kanjeng Cokro Sentono
Di nDalem Suryamentaraman Ngayogyakarta
Waktu jaman saya masih bocah
saya kelon sama simbah wedok
Dan saya mendapat banyak piwulang
apabila hendak tidur waktu malam
Lha ya, menyangkut banyak hal
Budi pekerti dan tata krama
unggah-ungguh dan suba sita
Bahasa Jawa yang bertingkat:
Berbeda tempat penggunaannya
—empan papan namanya
tergantung lawan bicara kita
Diselang-seling rengeng-rengeng
sebagai pengantar bobok saya
Simbah pun nembang Macapatan
suaranya tak hilang saya ingat
Walaupun giginya sudah ompong
dan ngomongnya sudah cedhal:
Sudah balik ke alam bocah
Tapi bagi saya jelas terdengar

Dongeng sejarah tanah Jawa
Sudah beribu tahun umurnya
Penuh gejolak, penuh peperangan
dan darah bersimbah di dalamnya
Bumi Jawa, o, bumi Jawa

menjadi ajang pertumpahan
Kerajaan demi kerajaan
berjaya dan tenggelam
Suatu masa bangkit—bertahan—
sudah itu musnah hilang
Bagaikan gelombang segara Kidul:
Pasang surut bergantian
bergantian pasang surut
Langka dicatat, langka dituliskan..."

The translation:

"Yes, yes, I am Pariyem
Maria Magdalena Pariyem in full
'Iyem' is my everyday name
From Wonosari in the Southern Hills.
I serve as a maid to his lordship Cokro Sentono
In the Suryamentaraman in Yogyakarta.
When I was still a little girl
I slept in the arms of my grandma,
I received many lessons
When we were about to sleep at night,
Well, about many subjects:
Good character and nice manners,
The right words to use and old sayings,
The levels of Javanese...
I still recall her voice
Although she had lost her teeth
And she talked in a funny way...

Tales from the history of the land of Java
Thousands of years old
Full of fire, full of fighting
And drenched in blood
Land of Java, oh land of Java
Was the scene of bloodshed.
Kingdom after kingdom
Flourished and fell
At a certain time, lasted,

Then was destroyed and gone
Like the waves of the Southern Ocean
Rising and falling in turn
Rarely noted, rarely written down..."

The lyrical prose of **Pengakuan Pariyem** was recited by the author before enthusiastic audiences of students, and this introduces us to the performance aspect of Indonesian literature, which is perhaps more important than its written aspect, and is found in such forms as the declamation of poetry, dramas modern and traditional, TV soap operas and pop songs.

Here is an example of a pop song lyric by the popular singer Iwan Fals.

Tikus-Tikus Kantor

Kisah usang tikus-tikus kantor
Yang suka berenang di sungai yang kotor
Kisah usang tikus-tikus berdasi
Yang suka ingkar janji
Lalu sembunyi di balik méja teman sekerja
Di dalam lemari dari baja
Kucing datang
Cepat ganti muka
Segera menjelma
Bagai tak tercela
Masa bodoh hilang harga diri
Asal tak terbukti ah
Tentu sikat lagi
Tikus-tikus tak kenal kenyang
Rakus-rakus bukan kepalang
Otak tikus bukan otak udang
Kucing datang
Tikus menghilang
Kucing-kucing yang kerjanya molor
Tak ingat tikus kotor
Datang mentéror
Cerdik licik
Tikus bertingkah tengik
Mungkin karna kucing

Pura-pura mendelik
Tikus tahu sang kucing lapar
Kasih roti jalan pun lancar
Memang sial sang tikus teramat pintar
Atau mungkin si kucing yang kurang ditatari

An old tale of office rats
That tend to swim in dirty rivers
A old tale of rats in ties
That tend to break their promises
And then hide behind the desks of colleagues
In cabinets of steel
The cat arrives
They change expression
Suddenly transform themselves
As if all innocent
Who cares if they lose self-respect
Providing there's no proof, eh
They'll surely swipe again
The rats are never satisfied
Greedy like nothing on earth
A rat's brain isn't a prawn's brain
When the cat arrives
The rats skedaddle
Cats that spend their time snoozing
Don't think about dirty rats
Coming to terrorize
Smart and tricky
The rats have spiteful ways
Pretend to glare
The rats know the cat is hungry
Give him bread and all goes smoothly
Yes it's bad luck the rats are so clever
Or maybe it's the cat isn't properly trained.

* * * * * * * * * *

This volume, though slim, has been wide-ranging and has tried to give an impression of some of the interesting aspects of the Indonesian language, in the hope that the reader will feel inspired to go on and pursue the subject further.

Some Suggestions
for Further Reading

The titles listed here contain materials relevant to the topics discussed above, as well as more titles in their bibliographies, for those who may wish to do further reading or carry out research.

Abas, Husen
1987 *Indonesian as a Unifying Language of Wider Communication; A historical and sociolinguistic perspective.* Pacific Linguistics Series D – No. 73. Department of Linguistics, Research School of Pacific Studies, The Australian National University, Canberra.

Alisjahbana, S. Takdir
1988 [1957] *Dari Perjuangan dan Pertumbuhan Bahasa Indonesia.* Jakarta: Dian Rakyat.

Anderson, Benedict R. O'G.
1990 *Language and Power; Exploring Political Cultures in Indonesia.* Ithaca/London: Cornell University Press.

Anwar, Khaidir
1990 *Indonesian – The Development and Use of a National Language.* Yogyakarta: Gadjah Mada University Press.

Aveling, Harry (ed. and transl.)
2001 *Secrets Need Words; Indonesian Poetry 1966-1998.* Athens: Ohio University Center for International Studies, Research in International Studies, Southeast Asia Series No. 105.

Aveling, Harry
2002 *Finding Words for Secrets; Reflections on the translation of Indonesian poetry.* Clayton: Monash Asia Institute, Working Paper 116.

Bellwood, Peter
1997 *Prehistory of the Indo-Malaysian Archipelago* (revised edition). Honolulu: University of Hawaii Press.

Blust, Robert
1987 'The linguistic study of Indonesia'. *Archipel* 34.

Braginsky, V.I.
1993 *The System of Classical Malay Literature.* Leiden: KITLV Press, KITLV Working Paper 11.

Campbell, Stuart
1996 'The distribution of -*at* and -*ah* endings in Malay loanwords from Arabic'. *BKI* 152/1: 23-44.

Drewes, G.W.J.
1948 *Van Maleis naar Basa Indonesia.* Leiden: E.J. Brill. Inaugural lecture, University of Leiden.

Errington, J. Joseph
1998 *Shifting Languages; Interaction and Identity in Javanese Indonesia.* Studies in the social and cultural foundations of language no. 19. Cambridge: Cambridge University Press.

Foulcher, Keith and Tony Day
2002 *Clearing a space; Postcolonial readings of modern Indonesian literature.* VKI 202. Leiden: KITLV Press.

Goebel, Zane
2002 'Code choice in interethnic interactions in two urban neighbourhoods of Central Java, Indonesia'. *International Journal of the Sociology of Language* 158: 69-87.

Gonda, J.
1952 *Sanskrit in Indonesia.* Nagpur: Sarasvati Vihara Series Vol. 28.

Grijns, C.D.
1999 'Indonesian terminology and globalism'. L'horizon nousantarien, Mélanges en homage à Denys Lombard III, *Archipel 58.*

Da França, António Pinto
1985 *Portuguese Influence in Indonesia.* Lisbon: Calouste Gulbenkian Foundation.

Heryanto, Ariel
1995 *Language of Development and Development of Language: The case of Indonesian.* Pacific Linguistics Series D – No. 89. Department of Linguistics, Research School of Pacific Studies, The Australian National University, Canberra.

Hill, David T. (ed.)
1998 *Beyond the Horizon: Short stories from contemporary Indonesia.* Clayton: Monash Asia Institute.

Hooker, Virginia Matheson
2003 *A Short History of Malaysia: Linking East and West.* Crows Nest: Allen & Unwin.

Jones, Russell (compiler)
1978 *Arabic Loanwords in Indonesian.* Indonesian Etymological Project III, Cahier d'Archipel 2, SECMI Paris/ School of Oriental and African Studies, University of London.

Jones, Russell
Forthcoming *Chinese Loanwords in Malay and Indonesian: A background study.* Indonesian Etymological Project IV. University of Malaya Press.

Maier, H.M.J.
1993 'From heteroglossia to polyglossia; the creation of Malay and Dutch in the Indies'. *Indonesia* No. 56 (October).

Mulyono, Anton M.
1986 *Language Development and Cultivation; Alternative approaches in language planning.* Pacific Linguistics Series D – No. 68. Department of Linguistics, Research School of Pacific Studies, The Australian National University, Canberra.

Oetomo, Dédé
1991 'The Chinese of Indonesia and the development of the Indonesian language'. *Indonesia*, Special Issue.

Poedjosoedarmo, Soepomo
1982 *Javanese Influence on Indonesian*. Pacific Linguistics Series D – No. 38. Department of Linguistics, Research School of Pacific Studies, The Australian National University, Canberra.

Pur, S.
1989 *Kamus Bahasa Khas Kawula Muda*. Jakarta: Generasi Harapan.

Rahardja, Prathama and Henri Chambert-Loir
1988 *Kamus Bahasa Prokem*. Jakarta: Grafitipers.

Ricklefs, M.C.
2001 *A History of Modern Indonesia since c. 1200*. Basingstoke: Palgrave.

Robson, Stuart
2002 *From Malay to Indonesian: The genesis of a national language*. Working Paper 118. Monash Asia Institute, Monash University, Victoria, Australia.

Robson, Stuart
2002a 'Dutch loan-translations in Indonesian', in Adelaar, K. Alexander and Robert Blust (eds.): *Between worlds: linguistic papers in memory of David John Prentice*. Canberra: Pacific Linguistics.

Skinner, C.
1978 'Transitional Malay literature: Part 1, Ahmad Rijaluddin and Munshi Abdullah'. BKI 134/4: 466-487.

Skinner, C.
1982 *Ahmad Rijaluddin's Hikayat Perintah Negeri Benggala*. VKI 22. The Hague: Martinus Nijhoff.

Sneddon, James Neil
1996 *Indonesian Reference Grammar*. St Leonards: Allen & Unwin.

Sneddon, James Neil
2000 *Understanding Indonesian Grammar; A students' reference and workbook*. St Leonards: Allen & Unwin.

Sneddon, J.N.
2001 'Teaching informal Indonesian: some factors for consideration'. *Australian Review of Applied Linguistics* 24/2: 81-95.

Sneddon, J.N.
2002 'Variation in informal Jakartan Indonesian: a quantitative study'. *Linguistik Indonesia* 20/2: 127-157.

Sneddon, James
2003 *The Indonesian Language; Its history and role in modern society.* University of NSW Press.

Steinhauer, Hein
1994 'The Indonesian language situation and linguistics; prospects and possibilities'. *BKI* 150-IV: 755-784.

Suryadi AG, Linus
1981 *Pengakuan Pariyem; Dunia Batin Seorang Wanita Jawa* [*The Confessions of Pariyem; The inner world of a Javanese woman*]. Jakarta: Sinar Harapan.

Suryadinata, Leo
1991 *Comparative Dictionary of Malay-Indonesian Synonyms.* Singapore/ Kuala Lumpur: Times Books International.

Teeuw, A.
1979 *Modern Indonesian Literature* (Volumes I and II). Second edition. The Hague: Martinus Nijhoff.

Teeuw, A.
1998 *De Ontwikkeling van een Woordenschat; Het Indonesisch 1945-1995.* Mededelingen van de Afdeling Letterkunde, Nieuwe Reeks, Deel 61 no. 5, Koninklijke Nederlandse Akademie van Wetenschappen (Amsterdam).

Vikør, Lars S.
1988 *Perfecting Spelling. Spelling discussions and reforms in Indonesia and Malaysia 1900-1972.* VKI 133. Foris Publications.

Wolff, John U. and Soepomo Poedjosoedarmo
1982 *Communicative Codes in Central Java.* Data Paper Number 116, Southeast Asia Program, Department of Asian Studies, Cornell University, Ithaca, New York.

Abbreviations

BKI Bijdragen tot de Taal-, Land- en Volkenkunde
VKI Verhandelingen van het Koninklijk Instituut voor Taal-, Land- en Volkenkunde (Leiden)

Glossary of Indonesian Words

acap	often
adat	custom
adik	younger brother/sister
air	water (n.)
akan	will, going to (future)
akan/terhadap	towards, regarding
akhir	end
akibat	result
aksés	access (computer)
aku	I (informal)
alam	universe; nature
alamat	address (place of residence)
alat	tool
Alhasil, ...	As a result, ...
alinéa	paragraph
ambil	to take
anda	you (single, neutral/formal)
anggar	to estimate
anggaran	budget
anggaran negara	national budget
anggur	grape
angkatan	generation, class
anglo	brazier
antisipasi	anticipation
apa	what?
apakah	whether, if
aplikasi	computer application
arti	meaning
asal	origin, provided
asli	original
asrama	dormitory
atas	the top
atau	or
baca	to read
bagaimana	how?/in what way?/like what?

bahasa	language
bahasa daérah	regional language(s)
Bahasa Indonesia	Indonesian, the Indonesian language
Bahasa Malaysia	Malaysian Malay (also Bahasa Melayu)
bahasa persatuan	language of unity
bahaya	danger
bahwa	that (conj.)
bakal	will, going to
bakmi	noodles with pork
ban	tire (n.)
bandar	port
bangku	bench
bangsa	nation
bangun	to build/to wake, get up
banyak	many
bapak	father
baskét	basketball
batin	inner
batu	battery
bawa	to carry, bring
bawah	the bottom
bécak	pedicab
béda	different, difference
béha	bra
béking	backing
belakangan	recently
benda	object, thing
bendéra	flag
berapa	how many?/how much?
berjalan	to go, travel
berkunjung	to visit (followed by "to")
bernama (X)	to be named (X)
berpendapat	to be of the opinion
bertemu	to meet (followed by "with")
berumur	to be aged (so many years)
besar	big
bestik	beefsteak
bestik	steaks (also chicken)
biasa	usual

Biasanya, ...	Normally, ...
biaya	expenses
bicara	talk
bisa	can, able; poison
bloknot	note pad
bocah	kid
bon	bill
bonéka	doll
buking	booking, to book
buntutnya	finally, in the end
butuh	to need
capai	tired
cat	paint
catat	to note
cerita	story
ceroboh	careless
coba	to try
cuacanya	the weather
cuci	wash
daérah	area
daftar	list
dalam	in, within
dalam	the inside
dapat	to get, obtain
dari	from
dari sini	from here
darurat	emergency
datang	to come
delapan	eight
demonstrasi	demonstration
dengan	with
dengan tepat	exactly
derajat	degree
destar	head cloth
dewan	council, panel
di	in, at, on (mainly spatial)
di atas	on top (of), above
di bawah	under, below
di dalam	inside

di luar	outside
di luar kota	outside town
di sini	here (in this place)
di situ	there (in that place)
dia	he/she/it (neutral/informal)
dialék Jakarta	Jakarta dialect
doa	prayer
dokter	doctor
dorslah	carbon copy
droping	additional budget
dua	two
dunia	world
ébi	dried shrimps
ejaan yang disempurnakan	perfected spelling
empat	four
enam	six
engkau	you (single, informal)
flu	influenza, flu
formulir	form (to fill in)
gandum	wheat
ganggu	to disturb, bother
gara-gara	because of
gardu	guardhouse
garpu	fork
geng	gang
geréja	church
goyang	to rock, sway
gua, gué	I (informal only)
gudang	warehouse
guna	use
guru	school teacher
hadap	to face, front on
hadiah	gift
hak	right (n.)
hal	matter, thing
handuk	towel
harap	(a polite, formal imperative)
harga	price
hari ulang tahun	birthday

harta	property
harus	should, ought to, to have to
hasil	yield
haus	thirsty
héwan	animal
hikayat	long narratives of a romantic or epic nature
hit	very popular
hot	very sexy
hujan	rain, to rain
hukum	law
ibu	mother
ijazah	certificate
iklim	climate
ikut	also
ilmu	science
indehoy	to have a romp (sexually)
indoktrinasi	indoctrination
informasi	information
inovasi	innovation
insidén	incident
instrumén	instrument
intégrasi lintas-platform	cross-platform integration (computer)
invéstasi	investment
Ironisnya, ...	The ironic thing is, ...
isi	contents
izin	to permit
jajak pendapat	opinion poll
jam bicara	consulting hours
jaman	era
jangan	don't/do not
jarang	seldom, rarely
jaringan	computer net(work)
jatuh	to fall
jawab	answer/to answer, reply
jendéla	window
jéngkél	annoyed
juara	champion
judul	title (of book, article)

jung	junk, boat
kacamata	spectacles, glasses
kadang-kadang	sometimes
kakak	older sister
kala	when
kalau	if
kalian	you (plural)
kamar kecil	toilet
kamar	room
kami	we (exclusive)
kamu	you (single, informal)
kantor	office
kapal selam	submarine
kapan	when?
Karena itu, ...	For that reason...
karena	because
kartu	card
karya	work
kawin	married
ke	to (spatial only)
ke sini	here (to this place)
keberatan	objection
kécap	soy sauce
kecil	small
kegagalan	failure
kejahatan	crime
kéju	cheese
kekalahan	defeat
keluar	to go out
keluhan	complaint
kembali	to come back
keméja	shirt
kemenangan	victory
kemudi	to drive (a car)
kendati	although
keponakan	niece/nephew
keréta	carriage, cart
kerja	work
ketimbang	compared with

ketimbang	than
kirim	to send
kismis	raisin
kita	we (inclusive)
kitab	scripture, technical books on Islamic theology and law
klakson	horn (on vehicle)
kongsi	company, association
kontroversial	controversial
koordinasi	coordination
kualitas	quality
kubur	grave (n.)
kué(h)	cake
kuli	manual laborer
kuliah	(university) lecture
kutang	brassiere
kwitansi	receipt
lahir	born
lamar	to apply, propose
langgar	chapel
lantaran	because of
layar	computer screen
lélang	auction
lemari és	refrigerator
lemari	cupboard
lici (léci)	litchi
lima	five
loténg	second floor of a building
lu	you (informal only)
lumpia	spring roll
lumrah	normal, common
maaf	pardon
mahal	expensive
Maka, ...	And so, ...
mana	where, which place?/which (one out of several)?
mandor	overseer
manut	obedient, docile
masuk	to go in

mau	to wish, want
médali	medal
méja	table
mémori	computer memory
menaikkan	to raise
mengairi	to irrigate
mengapa	why?/for what reason?
mengembalikan	to bring/send back
mengemudi	to drive (car)
mengobati	to treat (medical)
menjatuhkan	to drop
mentéga	butter
meréka	they
mesin maya	virtual machine (computer)
mesjid	mosque
meski(pun)	although
meskipun	although
mi	noodles
minggu	week, Sunday
minta	to ask for
mirip	to resemble
misal	example
miskin	poor
mohon	to ask for (formal)
muat	to hold, carry, contain
muda	young
mudah	easy
mula	beginning
Mulanya, ...	Initially...
mungkin	possible
murah	cheap
murid	pupil
musim	season
naik	to go up, rise
nakhoda	ship's captain
nama	name
nanti	soon, shortly
Natal	Christmas
negara bagian	state

negara	state
nikah	to marry
nisan	gravestone
Nusantara	Indonesia (literally "The Islands")
nyonya	lady, Mrs
obat	medicine
oléh	by
oléh karena	because of
omong Jakarta	Jakarta speech
pahlawan	hero
palsu	fake
pamor	shine, luster
panggil	to call, summon
panitia	committee
paro	half
pasar	market
pasién	patient (n.)
Paskah	Easter
pasok	to supply
pekan	week
pelajar	(school) student
pelan-pelan	slowly
pélek	rim (of bicycle wheel)
peluru	bullet
pembébasan	release
pemerintah	government
pemimpin	leader
péna	pen
penasihat	advisor
pengemudi	driver
pengisap debu	vacuum cleaner
pengobatan	treatment
peniti	pin
penjualan	sale
péntil	valve (in bicycle)
penyedia jaringan	computer server
peralatan	equipment
perang	war
perangkat lunak	software

perangko	stamp
perékonomian	economics
pergi	to go
perisai	patch (for computer; literally "shield")
perkamusan	lexicography
perlu	must, to need to
perlu	necessary
pérs	the press
perséro	(business) partner
pertama kali	first time
pesan	order
pesawat terbang	aircraft
pésta	party, feast
pikir	to think
pipa	pipe
pit	brush (pen)
pita	ribbon
pohon	tree
pohon-pohon	trees, trees (in general)
polis	policy (insurance)
polisi	police
potlot	pencil
prapatan	crossroads
primordialitas	primitive condition
produksi	production
profési	profession
prokem	"secret" argot, slang
proporsional	proportional
prosédur	procedure
puasa	to fast
pulang	to go home
pulpén	fountain pen
rahasia	secret
rapat	meeting
rasa	to feel, sense
rédaksi	editorial staff
reformasi	reform
rekan	colleague
rékayasa	to engineer, organize, fix

rembuk	to discuss, confer about
rendah	low
répétisi	rehearsal
réputasi	reputation
rilis	to release (song, product)
roda	wheel
ronda	night watch
rumah	house
rumah sakit	hospital
rupa	form, shape
rusak	out of order, broken
saat	moment
sabar	patient (adj.)
sabun	soap
sadel	bicycle seat
saja, sahaja	only; simple
saking	because of
saku	pocket
sama	same
sambut	to welcome, receive
sampan	boat
sana	over there (out of sight),
sasaran	target
satu	one
saudagar	merchant
saudara	you (single, formal)
saya	I (neutral/formal)
sahaya	I, servant
Sayangnya, ...	Unfortunately, ...
sebab	cause, because
Sebab, ...	This is because...
secara terbuka	openly, in an open way
sedang	is/are .... -ing (present continuous)
séhat	healthy
sejarah	historical work
sekarang	now
sekolah	school
sekolah dasar	primary school
sékrétaris	secretary

selalu	always
Selama ini, ...	Till now, ...
selamat	safe
semaksimal mungkin	as much as possible
sembari	while
sembilan	nine
sempat	to have the opportunity to
semua	all
senjata	weapon
sepatu	shoe
seprai	bedspread
sepuluh	ten
serba	all kinds of
serdadu	soldier
sering	often
setang	bar (in bicycle)
setéker	electrical plug
setip	eraser
setom	dryclean(ing)
setrik	hair ribbon
setrika	(to) iron
siapa	who?
silam	ago
sini	here, this place
sisa	leftover
sistém operasi	operating system
sistém operasi beragam	multi-operating system (computer)
situ	there, that place
soal	problem
solusi	solution
soré	afternoon
sosialisasi	socialization
stéker	(electrical) plug
stoplés	stoppered glass jar
stress	stressed
strongking	pressure lamp
sudah	already, has/have ... -ed (past or perfect tense)
sukar	hard

sumber	source
supaya	so that
suratkabar	newspaper
syair	a genre of poetry
tadi	just now, a little while ago
tahu	bean curd
takhta	throne
tamasya	picnic
tandatangan	signature
tanpa	without
taogé (taugé)	bean sprouts
tatabahasa	grammar
tauké	employer
téh	tea
téknologi informasi	information technology
telah	has/have ... -ed (past or perfect tense)
tembang	song
tempat	seat (on bus, plane)
témpo	time
tenaga	staff member
ténda	tent
tengah	in the process of
tentara	army
terasa	to feel (have a sensation)
terbuat	made (not known by whom)
terhormat	respected
terigu	wheat
teringat	to recall, remember
terjadi	to happen
terjemah	to translate
terkejut	to be startled
terkenal	well known
terletak	located
terlibat	involved
tersebut	aforementioned
tersenyum	to smile
tertanggal	dated (e.g. a letter)
tertarik	interested
tertawa	to laugh

tertelan	swallowed by accident
tertidur	to fall asleep
tertulis	written (not oral)
terusan	canal
tetangga	neighbor
tetapi	but
tidur	to sleep
tiga	three
tinggi	high, tall
tinta	ink
toko	shop
tua	old
tuduhan	accusation
Tuhan	God
tujuh	seven
tukang	craftsman
tulis	to write
tutur	to say
ubin	floor tile
ujar	to say
ulangan	test (in school)
umum	common, general
umur	age
undang-undang dasar	constitution
Uniknya, ...	The unique thing (feature) is, ...
upacara	ceremony
upaya	effort
usai	over, finished
wadah	container, umbrella organization
waktu	time, when
walaupun	although
warganegara	citizen
wawancara	to interview
yakin	certain
yang lalu	ago

COLLOQUIAL/SLANG WORDS

aja	only
akhirnya	finally, in the end

banget	very
baru-baru ini	recently
bikin	make
bokap	father
dapet	get
daripada	than
denger	to hear
doi	he/she, boyfriend/girlfriend
entar	later, soon
gimana	how? what?
gini	like this
gitu	like that
gua or gué	I
habis	over, finished
juga'	also
kali	perhaps
kalo	if, that (introducing a clause)
kata	to say
kayak	like (similar to)
lu	you
mémblé	lousy
met	with
muter	to play (a tape)
nangkering	to sit up high, perch
narik	to drive (car, bus)
nemenin	to keep someone company
nemuin	to find, meet
ngetop	to go to the top
nggak	no, not
nih	this
ntar	later, soon
nyokap	mother
ortu	parents
pada	(marking a plural, placed in front of the verb)
péngén	to want to
sama	with
sambil	while
sedang	in the process of

seneng	happy
snel	quick
so	so
tuh	that
udah	already (past tense)